THE BOOK
DAD
TOLD ME
NOT TO
WRITE

YOU CAN RUN A BETTER
BUSINESS WITH THESE SIMPLE
WORDS OF WISDOM…

RUSS HUGHES

Dedicated to my father, Gordon Hughes, who showed us that anyone can be a success and why so many fail to be. Dad died in 2021 after a short illness. This was the book he told me not to bother writing.

Forward

Sometime during 2019, I called Dad and suggested we should write a book to help all those running a business, based on all the wisdom he'd imparted to me over the years. I own two successful businesses - a blog I began in 2008, that today has millions of readers, and a specialist marketing agency that works with some of the best brands in the music and audio technology industry. I know that neither would be as successful as it is now, without the wisdom Dad passed on to me over the years.

But Dad's response was typical:

"We'd be wasting our time," he said.

Dad was always blunt and to the point. He had all the subtlety of a sledgehammer. When he said something, he was certain of it. In fact, his certainty was unnerving (though, at the same time, strangely reassuring).

I asked him why.

The response he gave is the exact reason why I wanted to write this book. It was a moment of wisdom. Not one wrapped up in lengthy dialogue that would instantly be forgotten, but a pithy one-liner, like the hook of a great song or the punchline of a joke.

"I can't put my head on their shoulders," he said.

I asked him to explain, even though I almost certainly knew what he meant. He went on...

"You can give people all the advice in the world, but most of them won't live it - and I can't do it for them."

He was right.

The world doesn't need another self-help book, and if people took notice of simple wisdom, we'd need a lot less of them. Plenty of people quote those books, but they don't actually apply the principles to their lives.

However, I believe we do need *this* book.

It's full of values that will cause you and your business to thrive if you take them to heart and practice them. But it takes a blunt, no-nonsense approach to delivering the truth - just like Dad.

So here it is, the book I was told not to write, filled with one-liners of wisdom. Will you prove Dad wrong?

Unforgettable, or How This Book Was Born

"I just can't get you out of my head."
Kylie Minogue

I think it happens to us all when we reach a certain age, but I have a problem when it comes to music. I can always recall *part* of a song, but never all of it. There are days when I walk around the house, singing one line of a song over and over - much to the annoyance of my family. Imagine hearing the lyric, *"The long and winding road..."* sung repetitively by me for two hours solid! I think you get my point. Perhaps you suffer with this too?

Why does it happen? The song is memorable enough to get under my skin, but not enough to embed itself entirely. I don't think this can be down to age, because my family have been laughing at me about it for years. As an aside, my wife has an equally annoying habit: I start singing a song, then she joins in, but in a different key! Not out of tune, just in a completely different key, as if every song is meant to have a power ballad key change, even at the end of the first line. I'm loathed to raise the issue with her as I like my bed too much. Some things are better left unsaid.

I digress...

There are some songs that stay with us for life, like *Happy Birthday*. I doubt there are many people on the planet from 3 to 103 that don't know all the lyrics to that song.

What's the hook?

Songwriters have a term for the part of a song that grabs you. For obvious reasons it's called the *hook*. It's the part that has you humming or whistling along. Invariably, *this* is the part of the tune that gets stuck in the mind; the bit we sing back to someone when we're trying to remember what the song is called.

Recently, science has given this part of a song a name: an *earworm*. Entire university departments are spending time researching the topic. *The Scientific American* wrote this in a November 2015 article:

"If you are one of the 92 percent of the population who regularly experience earworms–snippets of music that pop uninvited into your head and won't go away–you might wish there was a way to make them stop. Earworms are a generally benign form of rumination, the repetitive, intrusive thoughts associated with anxiety and depression." [1]

I'm not sure if Dad did it intentionally, but he had a way of expressing the business equivalent of an earworm. You would be in the middle of a discussion with him about some issue and out would come a nugget that

---

[1] Harriet Brown, Scientific American on November 1, 2015

would lodge itself in your brain. From that moment onward, it would stay there as a reminder.

This book is a collection of those lines. There are many here that Dad used during his life, and some others that I've thought of myself, or picked up along the way.

Regarding the latter, I'm not sure who came up with them first. I mention this because neither Dad nor I would want to take credit for moments of genius that were never ours in the first place. All I know is that these business hooks are used regularly in meetings with my team or with clients, and they are valuable enough to pass on to you.

Attention span

One-liners are a great way of delivering the truth with a punch. I'm not always good at reading. I think the internet has ruined my ability to concentrate, so I find myself reading the same line of a book over and over because I get distracted. It's the same with newspapers, magazines and even web pages. I start reading and, before I know it, I've zoned out. Perhaps you are the same; it's something that really annoys me about myself. My wife can immerse herself in a book for hours and stay completely focused. I, on the other hand, have the attention span of a puppy.

In his 2010 book *The Shallows*, Nicholas Carr suggests that the internet is changing the way we think, read and remember. In his words,

"The Shallows is not a manifesto for Luddites, nor does it seek to turn back the clock. Rather it is a revelatory reminder of how far the internet has become enmeshed in our daily existence and is affecting the way we think."[2]

Ironically, when I went to my bookshelf to remind myself of something from this book, I found it to be another unfinished read. The spirit is willing, but the flesh is weak!

I think this is why I find Seth Godin's books so helpful. He embeds nuggets of wisdom in chapters that are sometimes no more than a couple of pages long. His books defy the idea that in order to convey wisdom, you need to make it a long, drawn out affair. That's my kind of book!

Now for the good news

If you're the same, I have some good news for you. You should be able to read the chapter headings from this book and still capture the core lesson that the entire chapter goes on to explain.

My desire is that each of these one-liners become business *hooks* or earworms that you recall each day, and which help you to make better decisions. The aim is for them to be unforgettable gems which, when applied, make a huge difference to your business and life.

---

[2] The Shallows, Nicolas Carr, Atlantic Books 2010

I know they work because I use them every day in my business myself. If you try them out, you'll quickly realise how effective they are when colleagues and clients start quoting them back to you.

Who is This Book For?

"The measure of intelligence is the ability to change."
Albert Einstein

Possibly not you.

Dad was convinced that most people wouldn't follow through with the advice given. You might prove him wrong. Only time will tell, but here's a simple fact: if you stop reading now, then you won't. I wasn't supposed to write this book. Dad thought I was wasting my time and perhaps he'll be right again!

When I suggested to my late father that we compile a book of business advice, the idea received short shrift. The entire conversation, from pitch to push back, lasted no longer than five minutes. Dad wasn't one to waste time, especially on things he thought were a bad idea.

To get an idea past Dad took some work. Most ideas were shot down in flames as soon as they were mentioned. Some people would call it pissing on your fireworks, but with Dad there was rarely time to light the fuse!

You may be reading this thinking, *that sounds like a nightmare*!

Isn't it enormously frustrating to have conceived an idea and then pitch it, only to be told it's a bad one? For some it would be, but Dad was being brutally kind.

17

When it came to making decisions, Dad had little time for sentimentality. It was either going to work or not. I recall times when, as I got older, I'd ask him to humour me. He would, yet nine times out of ten he would still be right. It was infuriating!

One thing is sure, Dad didn't suffer fools gladly. He could spot a bullshitter a mile away. Suffice to say, his attitude was do it or don't.

Is this book for you?

So, who is this book for? Can you identify with one of the following statements?

- You want to run a successful business and find fast ways to improve performance
- You want the benefits without necessarily having to read the entire book
- You are easily distracted and are looking for quick ways to learn important lessons that can help change your business for the better
- Like me, you have the memory of a goldfish
- You're someone who didn't make it into a top business school, or you did and found that it really didn't help
- You have a pile of unfinished self-improvement books and don't want this to be another. (Can I break that curse?)

If you can answer yes to one or more (possibly all) of the above statements, then this book is for you.

Magic not included

There is one caveat. This book isn't magic. It's certainly not the only word/last word on many of the subjects covered. Rather, it's my version of them, peppered with many of the lessons gleaned from Dad over the decades.

I'm sure you've heard the old joke: How many therapists does it take to change a lightbulb? As many as you like but the lightbulb has got to want to change!

You have got to want to make a change and put in the effort to reap the rewards of the business wisdom here.

That said, I hope this book can bring you some new insights and that I'm able to convey them in a way that helps you to apply them for lasting good.

How to Read This Book

'The art of being wise is the art of knowing what to overlook."

William James

It's clear that when it comes to absorbing information there's not a one-size-fits-all model. I have a limited attention span. I'm also busy running two businesses and have a family with a small daughter and a dog who needs an hour of exercise a day. That's the dog, not my daughter!

Can I get you past page 18?

The writer Ashwin Sanghi says,

"The average buyer in a bookshop spends 8 seconds on the front cover and 15 seconds on the back cover before deciding whether to purchase the book or not. On average, he does not get past page 18. See? The odds are stacked against us writers!"

They say you can't judge a book by its cover, but it seems most people do. As you can surmise, there are plenty of people who want a fast fix or a shortcut. They make up their mind in less than 30 seconds and it appears that they don't get that far through any book. It would be depressing if that were the case with this book. It would be a waste of my effort and a waste of your money.

So, can I offer you shortcuts?

As part of my research for this book, I looked up quotes on shortcuts and I found a trend in most of them. They all suggested that shortcuts were a bad idea; that, in the end, they would lead to more problems. You may happen to agree.

This led me to do a bit more research on the perils of shortcuts (ironically using Google, rather than taking a trip to the library and scanning through pages of books for hours).

I found an article in a highly respected business publication that claimed to give six reasons why shortcuts were a bad idea and said that it had the research to back up this assertion. Yet, I found the examples somewhat dubious and the entire article lacking any *real* research to back up its claims.

In fact, the article seemed to be confusing the issue of *maintaining integrity* with *taking shortcuts*. I'm not convinced they are the same thing. I happen to think it's perfectly possible to maintain one's integrity while finding smart ways to do things faster. If at this point you too think that I'm using the word "shortcut" as a synonym for "compromise", that's not what I'm suggesting at all.

I'm not one to believe in overnight success. Both my businesses have taken over a decade to build. Both my father and I only started to find success when we were in our forties. We worked hard at many ventures before that. Some were bad ideas and failed. Speaking for myself, in my younger years I did plenty of things in an effort to make a business that were a bad idea, because I lacked either the skills or the discipline to follow them though.

It takes time to grow a strong, healthy business. Or, as someone has put it (it's been attributed to Jeff Bezos, Tom Clancy and Eddie Cantor),

"It takes ten years to become an overnight success."

If that is the case and the journey to success is a long one, then surely it would be smart to find as many valid shortcuts as possible? Only a fool would take the long route for a journey if there were a shorter one. Who jumps in a cab and asks the driver to take the long way around?

I work in an industry that relies heavily on computers to create music, then edit and mix the audio. Many of my clients create cutting edge software for music creation and processing, and the issue of workflow is critical. To make the tools as efficient and smooth as possible, shortcuts are employed. Keyboard shortcuts, macros and other methods are an integral part of the process.

In the same way, I want to impart some complex business values as quickly and easily as possible. It would be somewhat odd if that meant spending pages having to explain each one of them.

Why this book may fail you

During the research for this book it became clear that books offering business advice often fail for a number of reasons:

- Some say they find these books only have one core idea - the rest is padded out by saying the same thing in different ways

- Others told me they thought these books were too full of hype, quoting lots of success stories without showing the failures

- There was also concerns with the "you can be better than everyone else" rhetoric of certain books

- People also commented that many business help books were too dry and not funny enough (I'll try and make this as funny as possible)

- Another concern was that such books can be too prescriptive

I'll try to avoid all of the above - if nothing else, just to get you past page 18!

One word of warning...

You may have realised that I don't think in a linear fashion. Therefore, this book doesn't always flow in a linear manner either! With that in mind, I want to offer you a number of suggested ways to read this book.

For some, the title of a chapter will be enough. This is the hook I want you to remember. I know this can work for some people because I do it all the time with my team and clients. One line is all it takes and boom!

For some, this won't be enough. You want to go deeper, so each chapter will unpack the hook and give illustrations to show how it has worked in my business life. Some chapters will be longer than others, but I promise not to pad things out.

I also hope to offer challenges that you can apply to your own circumstances. These will ensure that the hook moves from inspiration to application. If it doesn't, then it's no better than the average feelgood meme on social media.

Also, this isn't a novel. There are no plot-spoilers. The chapters can be read in whatever order suits you. You may want to take a dip into a chapter, then leave the book for a while. That's fine.

Pick and mix

In summary:

- Read a chapter title and let it spark your imagination; interpret it how you wish
- Read the quick takeaway; it may be enough
- Read a whole chapter
- Read the entire book in a day

Whatever works for you, do it.

As long as this book is useful and helps to build a set of strong business values that help you grow, I'll have done what I set out to do. So, relax, enjoy and be enriched! Just get past page 18!

His Head on Your Shoulders

"If your time to you is worth savin'
Then you better start swimmin'
Or you'll sink like a stone
For the times they are a-changin'."

Bob Dylan

We all know people who seem as sharp as a knife; those people who seem to have more than their fair share of wisdom. Why is it that some people simply seem to *know* what to do, in an instinctive way?

It has been said that *wisdom* is making the right decisions, and you make them because you once made bad ones. But what if you could skip the first step? Is it possible to become smart without having to make the mistakes in the first place?

Conventional thinking suggests that wisdom comes with age and experience. You sometimes hear an older person laughing at a younger person who is making a mistake, saying something like, "Give them a few years and they'll learn!" However, there are plenty of foolish people in their later years and some people just out of college who are wise ahead of their years.

Age *can* help us to make better decisions, and experience is a good mentor, but it can't be taken for granted that the older we are the smarter we get. What we really need is *wisdom*.

What is wisdom?

The concept of wisdom is a huge subject. This book is not an in-depth study of wisdom. I simply don't have the education, experience or data to support such a treatise, so any attempt would be unwise. See what I did there?

That said, I do think it's possible to find shortcuts to wisdom by learning from the mistakes of others. Most of us don't have to eat poisonous food, put our hands in a fire, or send a picture of ourselves naked to a work colleague to know that all of these things are a bad idea. Thankfully, someone else already did them for us, to show the consequences of such bad decisions!

Wisdom isn't just learning from the mistakes of others though - it's also learning from their good ideas.

James Clear, author of the excellent and highly recommended *Atomic Habits*[3] has a weekly email called "3-2-1 Thursday". In it, he shares nuggets of wisdom and it is subtitled, "The most wisdom per word of any newsletter on the web". In a recent email he said,

"If you never copy best practices, you'll have to repeat all the mistakes yourself."[4]

James is right. Finding examples of smart thinking and good ideas, then applying them to one's own life is a brilliant shortcut.

---

[3] Atomic Habits, James Clear.
[4] James Clear, 3-2-1 Thursday.

Are you able to do this?

What makes some people smarter than others? How can we spot who is more likely to adopt smart thinking? I'd like to suggest there is a way to determine who is going to be smart and who is not, irrespective of age.

That is how *teachable* a person is.

Being teachable is an attractive quality and being unteachable a real turn-off. Who wants to be around those who think they have all the answers and are unwilling to learn? Being teachable is a sign of maturity; it has nothing to do with how many times you've flown around the sun.

I recall being in a meeting some years ago that was planning for a Sunday church service. The minister, who to be frank, loved the sound of his own voice and could go on for hours, was talking about how important his slot in the service was. He would regularly ask, with passion, "Where's the *teaching*?" This was often read by the rest of the team as him asking when he would get his slot to perform!

However, on this occasion, as soon as he stopped talking, someone else in the meeting commented, "Surely what we need to ask is, are they *learning*?"
This statement stopped the meeting in its tracks. It was an insightful comment and it goes to the heart of the question at the beginning of this book:

Can I put my head on your shoulders?

The answer is yes, but it requires a number of steps...

Firstly, you need to ask yourself, *am I teachable?* Are you willing to learn? Are you willing to set aside your preconceived notions, your prejudices, your bad learning? If challenged to change, will you do it? Are you able and willing to become a sponge to mop up learning?

I hope so. But that's not enough.

Learning made easy

A sponge is only useful if there is some liquid to soak up, so there's a second part to this.

Am *I* able to convey ideas to help you build a better business and life in ways you can easily soak up?

Dad said he couldn't put his head on your shoulders. I happen to think he was wrong. In fact, I'm certain he was wrong. How do I know?

He put his head on my shoulders!

That does not guarantee he can put his head on yours, but I know that the outcome is not down to him, it's down to you.

I'm 54 and I've built two successful businesses based on the wisdom Dad imparted to me. I know it works.

However, I want to dismiss one notion before we continue and that is a romanticised vision of how that took place.

Some may picture Dad in a wood panelled library, filled with the teachings of history, a fire burning brightly in the hearth, sitting there like Gandalf the Great. That each week I'd go into his sacred room and he would spend hours imbuing me with knowledge, telling me stories of old and anointing me with the laying on of hands.

None of that took place.

The way Dad imparted wisdom was in the everyday, rough and tumble of conversation.

We might be talking about me taking on a new office or staff and Dad would break into one of his moments. He would want to know why I needed to make those changes; why I needed to incur those extra costs. Then, like the end of a joke he'd been setting up, out would come the punch line:

"Profit is what you don't spend!" Or,

"Reputation is tomorrow's profit."

Boom! There it was, a life lesson in a single line. I would hear it and think, *Of course, that's so obvious.* It felt like common sense.

How common is common sense?

It has been said that we shouldn't call it "common sense" anymore. If it was that common everyone would have it.

It's believed that common sense was first written about by Aristotle. It has since been explored by many philosophers through the ages, and common sense has always been regarded as something of great merit.

But here's the good news: you don't need to be a philosopher or a genius to have it. Dad came from humble beginnings. You can read more about Dad's story at the end of this book.

Similarly, I left school with barely any qualifications, but both Dad and I managed to build successful businesses and very comfortable lives.

What follows is for those who want to build a successful business using gems of wisdom, without the need to understand complicated concepts that have eluded scholars for hundreds of years.

It is for those who may not have had the best start in life or the education they wished for.

Dad proved that success has little to do with upbringing, wealth or education. All those factors were stacked against him, but he found a way to win against the odds.

Dad had the ability to condense complex business ideas into one-liners. If you are willing to learn then I believe he can put his head on your shoulders.

Are you willing to try? If so, let's get started!

Reputation is Tomorrow's Profit

QUICK TAKEAWAY
"Reputation is tomorrow's profit"
What you do today increases or reduces your reputation, and that has a bearing on your future business. Work hard to cultivate and guard your reputation.

'Regard your good name as the richest jewel you can possibly be possessed of - for credit is like fire; when once you have kindled it you may easily preserve it, but if you once extinguish it, you will find it an arduous task to rekindle it again."

Socrates

It is something of an irony that while my company, Sociatech, spends its time working in marketing, we don't do any ourselves. Clients ask us to come up with effective, ingenious ways to help them market their products and services, but for us it's different.

It's not what is sometimes described as a "painter's house" or "mechanic's car" scenario. You know the score: the painter makes everyone else's house look amazing, while their own is in desperate need of decoration. The mechanic keeps your car on the road, but drives around in an old banger that can barely get started. So, it's not that we take care of others' business but not our own.

We don't go looking for work, because work comes looking for us. We regularly get enquiries from prospective clients asking if they can work with us. Would it surprise you to learn that we often have to turn work away?

The most common enquiry we get via email usually contains a line such as, "We have been looking for someone to help us make this happen and we asked around and were told we had to speak to you."

What is even more amazing is that these recommendations sometimes come from people we haven't worked with - they are simply passing on what they've heard from others.

Where is all the work coming from?

So, where is all this work coming from and how is it happening without us making any effort?

Word of mouth.

Entrepreneur defines it like this:

"Word-of-mouth advertising is important for every business, as each happy customer can steer dozens of new ones your way. And it's one of the most credible forms of

advertising because a person puts their reputation on the line every time they make a recommendation"[5]

Reputation is something worth investing in. It is to be guarded as one of the most valuable assets your business has.

There are some practical ways your business can engender the same kind of trust:

- Deliver on time
- Deliver on budget
- Deliver on your promises
- Keep your word
- Go beyond client expectations
- Be consistent

Genius isn't enough

Everything in the list above seems like a simple, practical thing, doesn't it? There's a reason for this. Let me expand...

I know and have worked with one of the most talented video creators on the planet. I also regard him as a good friend. His work is on-point every time. His content and presentation is faultless. He would be my first choice every time.

But there's one problem.

---

[5] entrepreneur.com

He is unreliable and inconsistent. He makes promises and doesn't deliver. He's been known to go AWOL (absent without leave) mid-project.

That problem becomes my problem because it impacts me and therefore my clients. It affects *my reputation* as well as his. That's the reason I am no longer able to use or recommend his services and I think that's a real shame.

Furthermore, his reputation for letting people down has spread. It's known by others. His reputation goes before him and not in a good way.

Genius is great, but if you fail in the small, simple things then it counts for very little on the road to success.

How I damaged my reputation

My realisation that a good reputation was essential to the survival of my business started around 35 years ago.

Rewind to the mid 1980s. I was in my early twenties and the Manager of a Pro Audio department in a large regional music store in the United Kingdom. I remember exactly where I was when I got a lesson that changed my attitude and set me firmly on the road to cultivating a good reputation.

I was driving back from London with my boss and friend, David Gregory. We had spent the day visiting a supplier, the then iconic mixer manufacturer, Soundcraft. At the time, David owned a black Porsche 911. It was the 80s, so although Porsche was a luxury car brand, the build quality and sound proofing weren't exactly up to today's standards! Although we were driving along in a head-turner, it was noisy at 70(ish)mph. It was getting late in the day and the sun was setting as we headed back to Birmingham.

"Russ," David said. "I need to have a chat with you about something."

I knew immediately it was one of THOSE conversations.

I started to get hot and my mouth went dry. I half-wanted to hear his next words and half not.

"OK," I ventured.

David told me that during our visit, the boss of Soundcraft had taken him aside to tell him that he loved working with us, but that I had a "reputation" amongst his team. More than that, I was gaining a reputation in the wider industry, and not the kind to be proud of. In short, he told David that it was damaging his business.

For David to tell me this was hard for him, and I knew he took no pleasure in having to convey this information. He said that people thought I was talented, knowledgeable, and an asset to the business... BUT!

He told me he had often heard the same thing from others and that the most important thing I needed to do was remove the "BUT" from the opinion people had about me.

Nearly forty years on, that conversation is as real today as the day it happened. It changed the course of my life in terms of reputation. Looking back, I have to acknowledge that I let my mouth run away with me in my 20s and 30s. I'm amazed I still have any of my own teeth.

It is said that losing one's reputation is like plucking a chicken in the wind. It's impossible to go back, pick up the feathers and push them back in.

Inside out

Reputation starts internally.

For us to cultivate an excellent reputation, we have to fix the unseen - the stuff we do when no one is looking. It's to do with making sure we have a strong internal core. After all, what people see on the outside is only a reflection of what is happening on the inside.

Much of the work we do at Sociatech is helping clients manage their reputation. This can happen before, during or after a product launch. It can happen at any point in the lifetime of a brand. As far as we are concerned, it's easier to prevent damage than it is to fix it. As medical professionals say, prevention is better than cure.

For us to help a client protect their reputation, we have to consider all the possible ways in which their customers and the wider public could perceive the decisions they make. As we consider any messaging the client is making, explicit or implicit, we examine the ways in which it could be misunderstood, misinterpreted or misrepresented.

We are trying to see problems before they happen. This can often mean we talk through scenarios and the likely consequences of saying one thing as opposed to another. Sometimes it means saying *something*; on other occasions it means staying *silent*.

There's a proverb found in the Old Testament of the Bible: "Even a fool can appear wise if he keeps his mouth shut." Sometimes the best way to protect our reputation is to stay silent. I'd go as far to say that oftentimes silence is the best policy.

What I hope is becoming clear so far, is that gaining a good reputation is an active process not a passive one. Cultivating a good reputation for your business takes effort.

What are you values?

Here's an exercise. Consider the values your business is built upon. If you don't immediately know what they are, there's some work for you to do. Without values your business is like a boat without a rudder in a storm. You'll be taken in whatever direction the wind blows you.

There's no right or wrong list of values - they just need to be ones you can commit to. But, for starters, I'd like to suggest some values all good businesses should adopt.

- Honesty
- Truthfulness
- Respect
- Diversity
- Quality
- Accountability
- Collaboration

There's one thing I'd like to point out about the values I've just suggested. Notice that they can work both *internally* and *externally*.

Strong values which can be fostered internally and externally are the start of a good reputation. Not one built on spin, or one that lasts as long as the office is open, or only when people are looking, but one that is the DNA of your brand; intrinsically woven into everything you do at a cellular level.

That's attractive, both to those you want to hire and those who want to hire you or buy your products.

Remember the Socrates' quote from the beginning of this chapter? Creating a brand reputation is "the richest jewel you can possibly be possessed of". This means clearly defining your values, then applying them to your business.

You may wonder what a set of values looks like. It's not my place to impose values on *your* business. What I can do, however, is share the values used in one of my businesses, Production Expert. These values have been developed over several years and govern the way we treat those who work for us, our partners and our readers.

- We are a community that encourages experts to gather and share their knowledge and wisdom, some of whom are on the team
- We are here to help our community above all other things
- We need money to make this happen, but that's not what motivates us
- For this reason, we make as much content as we possibly can available for free
- We are original, we don't follow the crowd
- We are consistent. That means delivering high quality content regularly, no excuses
- We under-promise and over-deliver
- We only speak about what we know, and we don't know everything. If we can't speak with authority, we find someone who can
- We reward positivity and ignore negativity, be it internal or external
- We have our critics and the more influential we become, the more of them we have. But we don't let them sap our energy or distract us from our mission
- Integrity matters to us; we do the right thing, whatever the cost

I'm not going to talk about these values in detail. I think they speak for themselves.

Making a contract with yourself

It's important for you to write down your values as a reminder, both to you and those who work with you. Writing them down moves them from being wishful thinking to establishing a contract. Not in the legal sense of the word, but in the commitment sense of the word.

Do you have a set of values you are building your business on? It's likely you do, but you may never have taken the time to articulate them in writing. Even if you work for yourself, it's important to do this and make a contract with yourself.

A couple of years ago, I decided it was time to lose weight. I was determined to follow through on it. However, something became clear: unless I measured and recorded my progress, it was easy to slide. Once I made a contract with myself about how much exercise I would do each day and how I would control my food intake, things began to change.

I have an Apple Watch, and one of the features is a set of rings that measure how much exercise you have taken each day, how many calories you've burnt, and how many times you have stood up. The aim is to close all three rings every day. For me, those rings are set at 40 minutes of exercise, 1,000 calories burnt, and standing

12 times each day. To date, I've closed all three rings for over 500 days in a row.

Secondly, I installed an app on my phone to track all the food and drink I consume each day, with a target of consuming no more than 1800 calories per day.

You may be reading this thinking I'm some kind of health freak or obsessed. Not at all. I have come to the conclusion that unless I record things in a way that can be measured, and hold myself accountable to those things, I'm likely to slide the wrong way. By using this method, over an 18-month period, I lost 25% of my body weight. I continue to use both methods to ensure I don't put it back on again.

It's the same with business values.

Writing them down holds us accountable. It's a written contract, so we know if we've honoured it or broken it. Furthermore, it acts as a reminder whenever we have to make a tough call about a business matter. Values become our touchstone.

Elvis Presley said, *'Values are like fingerprints. Nobody's are the same but you leave them all over everything you do."*

Use your values to make decisions

Just this week, a member of the Expert team told a management meeting that the advertising program for one of our partners wasn't working. He told us that, in his view, it wasn't a good use of the partner's money. Furthermore, the partner just kept paying the bills - they weren't complaining.

You may recall one of the values of the Experts: "Integrity matters to us; we do the right thing, whatever the cost."

We discussed it and decided we had two options. Either we find a way to give the client a better return on their investment or we cancel the contract.

You may think that's insane. If the client isn't complaining, then what's the problem? If we cancel, we lose revenue.

However, there's nothing right about taking someone's money if you know it's not in their best interest. At some point they will realise this, and if you've left it for months or years then they are going to feel cheated. The result: your reputation is damaged.

It's easy to make decisions based on short term gains, but if you make decisions based on the long game - having the reputation of being a good business to deal with - it will always bring you greater gains.

Reputation is tomorrow's profit.

FINAL QUESTION

Have you defined and written down the
core values of your business?

It Only Takes a Mouth to Criticise

QUICK TAKEAWAY
"It only takes a mouth to criticise"
Anyone can be a critic.
It takes vision, courage and effort to be the
answer to a problem that others avoid solving.

"I'm starting with the man in the mirror,
I'm asking him to change his ways.
And no message could have been any clearer,
If you want to make the world a better place
Take a look at yourself, and then make a change."
Michael Jackson

It was November 11, 2008, when I made the decision to start the website that in 2020 had around 7.4 million visitors. I recall the day, several months after starting the blog, when I was amazed we'd had 1000 visitors in one day! I made my wife stay awake with me to see us pass that number. On many days now, we have more than that in an hour.

Today, it's a regular occurrence where I'll start a conversation with someone in the music or post industry and they'll ask, "Are you the Pro Tools Expert?" Then begins a slightly complicated conversation where I explain I *was*, but now I'm not. I'm busy doing other things and a fantastic team runs the Expert sites for me.

They let me write the odd article (internally called Russ' rants!) and it's not just about Pro Tools anymore.

I suppose I could simply say "Yes", but I think that makes things more complicated. If I could prime people to ask me if I am the guy who started it, that would make for quicker answers.

It's a conversation I've had recently with a sound engineer in a Belfast recording studio, with producer/engineer Dave Darlington in New York, and one of the marketing team at Eve in Berlin, Germany.

I've met people at weddings and was even stopped in a pub in London when someone recognised my voice from the podcast we produce. They had never seen my face, but then I've always had a good face for radio.

My daughters, who both live in London, have been on dates where the guy has found out their Dad is "the one who started the Experts blogs", so the conversation has turned to that. One of my daughters told me that on one date, once the cat was out the bag, the guy wouldn't stop talking about it. Apparently, he wanted to meet me. That would have been a disappointing moment for him. Suffice to say, he didn't get a second date either. Idiot!

I suppose this recognition is a sign of the enormous reach and impact the blogs have had, and is a sign of that somewhat nebulous term "success".

Another measurement of success is that around half a dozen people now make a living from the Expert sites and many more supplement their income from it. Even better, for the most part, the site is free for those who visit it, except for a small section of premium content which helps to supplement the income of the video authors. But making the content free was one of the core principles I laid down when I started the blog in 2008.

There wasn't a master plan

Here's the most significant fact: I never planned or imagined that the blog would garner the following it has, from hobbyists to Grammy-winning producers. I certainly never thought it would generate any income, let alone enough to keep the roof over a lot of heads.

The blog was no master plan. It was not started to make money and certainly not to be as hugely successful as it is today, as one of the leading web publishers in the audio technology industry. A few months ago, I had a conversation where someone described the site as a "juggernaut". It's come a long way in the last 12 years and has certainly exceeded any expectations I had for it.

It started for one reason. I was in a forum where people were moaning about how they weren't getting any support to use the products from the brand who made them. One person said, "Somebody should do something." When people say that, what they mean is anyone should do something but them.

It only takes a mouth to criticise.

As I looked at these comments, I wondered if I was the answer to the problem. I had some spare time and thought I might be able to help. I didn't know how, but I thought that if I could pass on some of the great things I'd learnt from the producers and engineers I'd been around over the years, it might benefit a few people. So, the blog began.

When I started the blog, I was simply another member of the forum. I had no contacts, no influence, no money and no mandate. I didn't have any coding experience. I didn't know the best way to make videos and share them with the world. I made everything up as I went along.

Sometimes the only qualification is willingness

It has been suggested that when Moses went up the hill to meet God and collect the Ten Commandments, he did so because no one else stepped forward. Often the highest qualification you can have to take on a task is the willingness to try.

It wasn't easy. During the early years I spent around 40 hours a week making videos, writing and maintaining the blog. This was in addition to a fulltime job. I worked on the blog from the moment I got home from work until about midnight, sometimes all night. I worked on it most weekends.

Emails I sent to brands were ignored. I tried to call in favours from those I knew who worked in the industry. Those requests were largely ignored too. In the first few years of the blog, the revenue was zero.

In the early years I made countless mistakes. Looking back, some of the first videos were awful. The articles contained typos and inaccuracies. I nearly got sued a few times and had to take stuff down. I recall one conversation with a large US brand where I had the Head of Marketing screaming down the phone at me, threatening me with lawyers. Oddly enough, I miss some of those early days. There was something maverick about it all. I think that's part of the attraction of pioneering.

I recall being in a meeting with a room full of traditional publishers, many of whom thought the blog was a joke. When we sat down to eat lunch, one of them decided he would belittle me in front of the table, telling me what I was doing wasn't how it was done; that I was breaking the rules.

I wasn't sure what to say, other than feel embarrassed and stupid. I didn't keep to any of "the rules" because I didn't know them in the first place. A decade on and half the publications in that room have gone, including the one run by the guy who thought it would be clever to belittle me in public.

What's your excuse?

When we see a problem, we have two choices: to complain and think someone else will do something about it, or to be the answer. We can make excuses about not having enough time, money or the right qualifications, but often that's all they are, *excuses*.

Greta Thunberg could have made the same excuses. A teenager, diagnosed with Asperger syndrome, obsessive-compulsive disorder, and selective mutism. What could she possibly achieve? I think we know the answer.

It's easy to think someone else will clear up the mess.

A friend of mine, the vicar of a small parish church in England, told me the story of an incident that happened to him a few years ago. One morning there was a knock at the vicarage door. When he opened it, he found a somewhat agitated member of his congregation.

Before my friend could speak, the man began to rant about how disgraceful it was that the door to the church was looking so tatty and in poor repair. It was, in his words, dishonouring to God and, "Someone should do something about it!"

My friend said he agreed and asked the man to wait for a minute. When my friend returned to the door, he handed the man a paint brush. The man left the church a few weeks later. He didn't paint the door.

"No one is useless in this world who lightens the burdens of another," says Mr Rokesmith to Bella Wilfred in *Our Mutual Friend*.[6]

In business, we are presented with problems all the time – both internal ones that arise as we run our business, and external ones from our clients; possibly too, the problems we find as we visit forums or social media.

The world is filled with problems. Being willing to try to solve them can not only transform the issue and the lives of those affected by it, it can change us.

The success of solving problems

The commercial imperative of any business is to solve problems; to be the answer people are looking for. Those who offer solutions are offering leadership and if you want to be a market leader then you first need to learn to be a business leader who is pioneering new or better ways to solve problems.

I was delighted to see a client of Sociatech, Synchro Arts, receive a technical Academy Award for Scientific and Engineering contributions to the film industry.

The Academy stated that "VocALign and Revoice Pro are software tools that together give sound editors unprecedented control over the final performance in replaced dialog. In use for many years, these

---

[6] Our Mutual Friend, Charles Dickens.

technologies continue their predominance in the creation and seamless integration of replacement dialog tracks in motion pictures."

Jeff Bloom, the CEO, has been a client and friend for nearly a decade, but the story of how he did it goes back 40 years. Synchro Arts' technology helps those working in pictures and sound to align vocals. The technology is based on the same stuff that helps guided missiles hit their target. As I've said to Jeff on many occasions, it really is rocket science.

Jeff saw a problem. When actors overdubbed lines to films in the studio after the shoot, the new recorded lines wouldn't line up with the ones recorded on set. He decided to figure out a way to solve this.

Several decades later, Synchro Arts are the industry leader. Their contributions to the industry have won them both Emmy and Academy Awards.

I'm sure Jeff didn't set out to be an industry leader, rather he decided to attempt to solve a problem. That took leadership. The rest, as they say, is history.

The empathy of problem solving

I've mentioned that my Dad's story is one of a bad start in life (you can read more about it at the end of this book). Suffice to say, the odds were stacked against him, not only as he was growing up, but later on in life.

Just after he married, he was taken into hospital and diagnosed with spinal tuberculosis. He spent a year in hospital receiving treatment until he finally came home. For the next decade he had to wear a back brace every day. It was like a saddle. I clearly recall the smell of leather and sweat as he took it off at the end of each day.

Despite the economic, emotional and health setbacks during the first few decades of his life, Dad didn't let this stop him from trying to solve problems.

In the early years of marriage, Dad attempted several business ventures with varying success. Things were financially precarious for him and Mum, trying to bring up four kids under five, but Dad decided life was about trying to make things better - not just for them, but for anyone he could help. Mum tells me that even though they were broke, one Christmas Dad went out and bought Christmas presents for a friend of his who couldn't afford to get them for his children.

Leadership is something that starts within us. It taps into the values I spoke about in the previous chapter. Dad decided that one of his values would be to find ways to help other people; to show generosity whenever he could. I'm absolutely convinced it was driven by the experiences of his early years. Despite growing up with very little, Dad was never the victim and he wanted to make sure others weren't either.

It comes as no surprise to me that he eventually found success in his business, selling commercial insurance, pensions and investments. He didn't want other people to worry about money like he had as a child and that's why he sold pensions and life cover.

He didn't want business owners to worry about fire, flood, theft or a multitude of other disasters that can face a business, that's why he made sure the insurance they got would protect them.

I recall several times when Dad went to war with an insurance company on behalf of a client. For Dad it was a matter of principle. They had paid for protection and peace of mind and Dad was going to make sure they got it.

That sense of wanting to do the right thing, wanting to solve people's problems, earned Dad enormous respect. I recall as I was growing up, whenever I was out with Dad, we'd be stopped in the street by people who knew him. Before you knew it, they were telling me how wonderful Dad was.

It felt like walking around with a famous person. We would walk into a butchers, a clothing shop, or the barbers and Dad would be treated like royalty. It was almost common knowledge that if you needed help, Dad was the man to ask.

Dad didn't help people for fame or the money, but it was great to see him get the recognition he deserved; to see his business flourish and provide him and Mum with a wonderful life.

Dad was a leader in the truest sense of the word, and he was rewarded for showing true leadership time and again.

Be the solution

The world isn't short of problems, it's short of problem solvers.

Which do you want to be, the person who thinks someone else should do it, or the one who decides to lead?

Leadership requires vision, courage and determination.

It only takes a mouth to criticise.

FINAL QUESTION

Is there a problem that needs solving that you've avoided being the answer to?

Scratch the Itch

QUICK TAKEAWAY
"Scratch the Itch"
Running a successful business is about solving problems. The better you are at taking away problems for other people, the more they will use your products and services.

"Problems are nothing but wake-up calls for creativity."

Gerhard Gschwandtner

My wife has given up trying to explain what I do for a living. If we're out and someone asks, she'll look at me, shrug her shoulders and say, "You tell them!"

If people ask me, I try and simplify the two things my businesses do. I work in technology marketing and have an online publishing business. That's an accurate description, but when you break any business down to its most basic level, we are really *problem solvers.*

The success of your business depends on how good you are at solving your clients' problems. That might be mastering an album, selling a plugin, removing an iron bar from their skull, painting their wall or walking their dog.

You might be reading this and hate to think that your profession can be reduced to such a simple transactional act, but it's really that simple. Solve the problems clients bring to you and they'll be happy. The better you are at doing it, the more they'll return. If you're good, they'll also recommend you and soon you'll have a reputation for being good.

When I'm asked by my team about this, I tell them to *find the itch and scratch it.*

Forget the how and focus on the why

Just before Christmas last year, for a treat my wife and I took our 5-year-old daughter to the McDonalds Drive Thru for lunch. We were in the middle of the COVID pandemic and all the restaurants were closed, so the queue for the Drive Thru was long.

As we sat waiting in the car, the song *Last Christmas* by Wham came on the radio. My wife was singing along to it, but my mind was somewhere else. I'd started to wonder if the snare drum on the track was a Linn Drum or a Drumulator - both iconic drum machines used on many records in the 1980s.[7]

Meanwhile, back in the car, my wife asked me what I was thinking about, so I told her. She looked at me as if I was mad.

---

[7] The question was answered later when I got home, it is a Linn Drum.

"You don't know what I'm talking about, do you?" I said.

"It's just a great tune that I love," came the reply.

The music and postproduction industry spend an inordinate amount of time discussing the gear it uses. It talks about the best products and how to use them. There are pages and pages of forum discussions about the very question I was considering. Discussions there often descend into all-out warfare as the keyboard warriors flame one another. It can get very nasty during a discussion about a drum machine or a microphone!

I've started to wonder recently if painters do the same thing, or car mechanics, or surgeons? Do they discuss, or worse, argue about the tools they use?

Our agency has made perhaps 500 product promotional videos for clients over the last few years. Clients have loved our work and we are proud of the creativity each one contains. However, I can't recall a single occasion when a client has asked me what gear we used to produce it. Most of them don't know which cameras and lenses we've shot the video with. They don't know if the computer is a Mac or a Windows PC. They don't know what software we've edited it with, or the plugins we've used. To be frank, I don't think they care.

What's more, the people watching the videos have no idea what gear was used and, again, 99% of them don't care.

No one buys a single because it has a great snare sound. No one watches a movie because it was shot with a Red Camera. No one hires a painter because of the paint brushes they use, or a mechanic for the toolset they have.

People just want us to fix their problems!

Too often, we are so obsessed with *how* we do our work that we forget *why* we do it.

I'm convinced that most of the people who spend their day talking shop in these forums can't be the ones making the money. The people making money are far too busy to spend all day discussing the tools of their trade.

So far, I've talked about how this applies to those offering a service like mixing, painting or healthcare, but the same principle extends to products too.

Let's RX It!

One of Sociatech's first clients was the hugely smart iZotope Inc. iZotope are a US-based software and hardware brand, making products for music and post professionals that perform a variety of tasks with audio. iZotope are leaders in their field and have come up with ingenious ways to solve complex problems in simple ways.

About 10 years ago, they came to me and asked if I could help them increase the awareness of one of their flagship pieces of software, iZotope RX. This software helps to remove a variety of sound problems like hiss, background noise and hum. It's very clever technology for dealing with audio issues.

As we considered the plan, I suggested we turn the name RX from a noun into a verb with the campaign, "Let's RX it!"

We worked on a series of videos to demonstrate how effective RX is at dealing with noise. The aim was to reinforce the phrase "Let's RX it!" The dozen or so videos consisted of challenges to remove issues such as hum, mobile phones going off mid-interview, and other everyday problems that sound engineers get thrown at them.

The videos were each around three minutes in length and showed the before and after, as well as how quickly the result could be achieved. They were fun to make and really hammered home the idea that if you had a problem, the best thing to do was RX it.

Today, iZotope RX is synonymous with solving problem audio. Trawl through social media and forums and whenever anyone asks what to use to fix noise on problem audio, you can bet the answer from those in the know is to use RX.

Problem solving makes you popular

Irrespective of the task at hand, problem solving makes you popular. Who doesn't want someone or something to make their problems go away?

You may be aware of the meme *good, fast, cheap*. It is said that a client can choose two of them, but you can't have all three. But imagine if you can make that work in your favour? What if you can offer a service or product that means clients are less sensitive to one of more of those metrics?

In my experience, most reasonable people are willing to pay a premium for quality and speed. The aim of any business is to eliminate the possibility of price being a barrier, or if nothing else, reducing its influence in the buyer's decision.

When I was in my twenties, I worked as a salesman in a car audio store. This was the kind of shop that sold car stereos and the associated equipment, costing hundreds if not thousands of pounds.

I had been working there a few weeks and had just finished serving a customer when the owner-manager of the store called me into his office at the back of the shop. He looked unimpressed.

"What did you do wrong with that last customer?" he asked

"I'm not sure," I replied (I didn't have a clue).

"You asked them what their budget was," he said.

I was confused. Surely that was one of the first questions you should ask?

"Find out what they want, then give it to them," he continued. "Even if they had a budget in mind, they'll exceed it if you enchant them."

Really? I thought.

"What's more," he continued, "when they're down the pub, they won't be telling their friends how you made them spend more than they wanted, they'll just be raving about their amazing new stereo."

When I first heard this, I thought it defied logic. I had always thought people were price sensitive; that this was the *first* thing on their mind.

When we solve people's problems - or better, when we exceed their expectations - price is not the first consideration. If we enchant them and put a smile on their face, they'll pay a premium.

At Sociatech, every time we have a new project for a client, I'm determined that we'll do it better and faster than they expect us to.

Beat the deadline and come in under budget every time, and make sure you deliver something that's even better than the customer expected.

These days we are rarely asked about the cost because our clients know our day rates and trust us to offer them value for money. I can't remember the last time a client questioned an invoice from us.

People hire us to solve their problems, whether that is through services or products. The better we are at doing it, the more work we will get. Furthermore, our clients will be less price sensitive if we excel at delivering.

FINAL QUESTION

Do you identify the issues before offering a solution?

What Are We Trying to Do?

QUICK TAKEAWAY
"What are we trying to do?"
Always make sure you know the purpose
of an activity before starting, otherwise
you may waste a lot of time.

"It is a mistake to think that moving fast is the same as actually going somewhere."

Steve Goodier

You may or may not be surprised to learn that many businesses, large or small, have no clear idea of what they are trying to do. Some have little idea where they are going, while many are unaware of where they have come from!

Terry Pratchett summed up the problem:

"If you do not know where you come from, then you don't know where you are, and if you don't know where you are, then you don't know where you're going. And if you don't know where you're going, you're probably going wrong."[8]

---

[8] Terry Pratchett, I Shall Wear Midnight

What's the problem?

Sociatech had been hired by a small software company to help them with their marketing. It's a common scenario we find ourselves presented with. I'm of the opinion that no one calls us unless there's a problem.

Our first call was with the Founder of the company, during which it became clear that he was frustrated with the performance of the business.

Our initial discussion with any potential client is used to gain a general understanding of the business. We ask about the company history, when it was founded and, more importantly, *why* it began. We ask about the current position of the business, what they do, the structure, who the main people are, to get a sense of the management. Then we ask about current and future plans for the business.

This first call can last anywhere between an hour to several hours. We act like business detectives, trying to understand the business in as much detail as possible. In our opinion, this knowledge is vital if we are going to be effective.

We do this for two reasons.

The first is to ascertain the state of the business. In some ways it's an ad-hoc SWOT analysis.

SWOT is an acronym for the process that examines the Strengths, Weaknesses, Opportunities and Threats of an organisation. SWOT is attributed to Albert Humphrey, who developed the process at the Stanford Research Institute in the 1960s to help formulate effective business and organisational strategies.

The second reason for this initial research is to ascertain if we can actually help the client. Not every opportunity is something we can get involved in for a variety of reasons.

Once we had conducted the initial consultation, it became clear that the Founder of the company didn't know what they were trying to do. Each member of the company was working hard and making some progress, but they had never decided what they were all trying to achieve *together*.

They didn't have a common purpose, a goal, or even values, so it didn't matter how hard they worked. How would they know if they were pulling in the same direction? Worse, how would they know if they were inadvertently working against each other?

You may be thinking, *how is it possible for people to be working in the same organisation and not know what they are trying to achieve?* It's possible because this can happen even when there's only one person running the business!

Later, in the chapter More Heat Than Light, I'll speak about how energy can be wasted when a person is doing the wrong job. Here, I want to talk about an equally damaging business failure: a lack of direction.

Baby you can drive my car

When our youngest girl was a baby, some days we would just jump in the car and drive. It was just for fun. We didn't know where we were going or how long we would drive for. The journey was an end in itself; there was no destination, just a journey.

Then there were nights when our baby girl cried so hard, we would try anything to get her to sleep. It was the kind of crying you think will never end! On those occasions, my wife and I would strap her into her car seat, start the car and just drive. At some point she would fall fast asleep. It could take a matter of minutes or, on the bad nights, an hour or more!

Then there was a third kind of journey - when we strapped her into her seat, got in the car and headed out to the beach, to visit friends or relatives, or to go shopping.

It was the same car, the same people, but each journey had a very different purpose.

The first journey was for leisure; to waste time together; to get on the road and see where we ended up. It didn't matter where we went.

The second journey had no destination, but it definitely had a purpose: to stop the baby crying. It still didn't matter where we went. What mattered was that we found peace!

The third journey had both a purpose and a destination. We knew where we were going, so we planned how to get there.

In business, it's important to know *why* you are taking the journey. It's unlikely you are in business just to while away the day, so running your business without a purpose and destination is a waste of time and money.

Perhaps your business has a purpose, but no clear destination. That's not entirely wrong, but how can you measure the success of your purpose without a goal?

That's why having both a *purpose* and a *destination* is essential when running a business. It allows you to set goals and know when you have reached them.

Let's say, for example, that you start a business to serve the TV and film industry by offering a professional service composing music. You begin the journey, but you don't have a clear, specific destination in mind. How will you know what success looks like if you don't have a target?

Hitting the target

Many of us avoid targets because we are afraid of failure. We think that if we set targets then miss them, we will become demotivated.

However, we all have targets even if we don't write them down. Even a one-person company has a target: make enough money to pay the bills! Targets don't only prevent failure, they encourage success.

When I started the Expert websites 12 years ago, I had a number of goals:

- Create high-quality, focused content
- Make as much material as possible free to the end user
- Remain independent

How did I measure the success of each goal? Some of the measurements were qualitative and some quantitative.

Right from the outset, I installed a visitor counter into the website with one aim: to see how people were responding to the content. If the content was good, then more people would visit. If they trusted us, they would visit. The great thing for visitors was there was no barrier to entry. They could consume most of the content for free.

I've been asked over the years how one creates a website that has over 7 million visitors per year. There are two parts to the answer.

The first part is simple, and that is to have a larger number of people visit the site than the day before.

In the early days, it was just me thinking, *yesterday we had 1,000 visitors, so tomorrow we need more than that.* Even if it was 1001, it was still a higher number. I've been doing that for 12 years now. Every day the number has to be higher than the day before.

Look at it this way. If I started with 1,000 visitors in 2008 and increased that by one visit per day, by 2021 I'd have over 5,000 visitors each day. If I increased by just 10 visitors per day, by 2021 I'd have over 40,000 visitors a day.

Little and often

What's so remarkable about this thinking is that the numbers don't represent some unattainable goal - they are small incremental gains. If I had decided in 2008 that I'd like to get 7 million visitors a year, I would have soon become demotivated. Even a target of 1 million would have felt like climbing Everest.

This is why initiatives like "Couch to 5K" are such a great idea. You don't jump off the couch and run 5K on day one, you walk to the end of the street. On day two you might walk and then run back. As each day passes, the goal gets harder. Within weeks, however, you are laughing at how hard it was to walk to the end of the street as you finish running 2K. Each day you reach a new milestone and each win becomes bigger.

I've lost weight, got fit and grown businesses all using the same method, but you have to have a goal. Without a goal, losing weight, getting fit or growing a business are nothing but a wish list.

It's not enough to say how much weight you want to lose; you need to say how much and by when. In business, you need to say where you want to go and by when. You might fail, and you won't always hit the target, but you are progressing towards a definite goal that can be measured.

I didn't hit the daily growth target every day with blog, but that didn't stop me wanting to. When I decided to get fit and run 5K, some days I would walk when I should have run. On other days, I didn't think I'd make the first 1K, but then find I'd beat my 5K time.

Without a goal you have less chance of making a change. With a goal, at least you know what you're trying to achieve. You might fail, in which case you can always move to plan B, but you need to have a plan A to begin with.

Comedian Spike Milligan is quoted as saying, *"We haven t got a plan, so nothing can go wrong!"*

I'm convinced some people genuinely think that's true. Sadly, it's not.

There are moments of luck in any venture. You happen to meet a client at a wedding who gives you a big contract. You win some work because your new client's usual supplier has let them down. There are serendipitous moments that happen to people in life, but they are the exception not the rule.

Hitting a target takes constant effort

For most, hitting targets is hard work. This brings me to the second part of the answer of how the Experts site became such a success.

I blogged every day. I never missed a day. In fact, some days I would blog two or three times. Nothing stopped me - not sickness, vacations or weddings - I would blog. My laptop never left my side. I've blogged in airports, while my daughter was taking her gymnastics class, in hospital while waiting to visit a loved one. I've blogged on Christmas Day. I think I even blogged on my wedding day!

I looked at the visitor numbers every day and knew that making sure the number went up depended on me consistently providing high quality content. The readers didn't know what was happening in my life, and I didn't expect them to. What I knew was, the bigger the blog became, the more people depended on the content being produced. Some people have told me it was the first site they visited each morning and the last one they read at night.

What if they visited some days and there was no new content? That meant they may not visit tomorrow... or ever again!

Goals aren't magic, they only happen if we commit to achieving or beating them.

Spiderman and Batman

Goals start with the asking of questions and the most fundamental one is "What are we trying to do?" The first answer you provide to that question may not be the real one. Let me explain...

There comes a point in every parent's life when their child starts to ask lots of questions. You can be driving along and suddenly your child will ask, "Mummy, which ice cream is the best? Chocolate or strawberry?" To be honest, that's an easy one. Wait until you get, "Daddy, if there was a fight between Spiderman and Batman, who would win?"

These questions are easy, but soon comes the day when every question starts with the dreaded *why?*

Why is the sky blue? Why can't penguins fly? Why did the dog die?

Sometimes they come at you like machine gun fire, and each of them deserves an answer.

Rudyard Kipling expressed it well in this poem:

> *"I keep six honest serving men*
> *They taught me all I knew*
> *Their names are What and Why and When*
> *And How and Where and Who."*

It's crucial that every business asks the vital questions.

Sometimes people are afraid to ask questions, especially in meetings. We wonder if it makes us look dumb. In my opinion, the person asking the questions is the smart one in the room. Let's consider this in a practical example.

A client calls me and asks that we make a new promotional video for a product. There are several fundamental questions we need to ask before we can even begin to consider the task. Here are a few...

- What is the product?
- Who is the target audience?
- What are the key messages that need to be conveyed?
- Is the product ready? When can we see it?
- Are there similar products on the market, and what are the benefits of this product?
- How much does the product cost?

- Who is supplying the assets, such as logos and other images?
- What is the budget?
- When does it need to be ready?
- Where will it be seen?

These are the most basic questions we will ask, so we are able to come up with an idea, a treatment and a budget.

However, even with that list of questions (which is by no means exhaustive) two questions remain to be asked:

- *Why* make a video?
- What will *success* look like?

I've seen some stunning, clever, beautiful, classy product videos during my career that, at the same time, were utterly useless in selling the product. No one had asked the important question: "What are we trying to do?"

It may be that once you find out what the client defines as success (normally expressed as a sales number), a video may not be the best way to achieve that result.

When we approach a task, it can be very easy to go on autopilot, because that's what we've always done, or because it's what everyone else is doing. It's important to stop, stand back and analyse the situation by asking the right questions.

The music industry is having to ask difficult questions right now about the streaming model. "Everyone is doing it" is perhaps why so many have rushed to get on platforms like Spotify. FOMO (the fear of missing out) may well be the reason many artists have made the choice to use the platform. Yet, few are making any real money from streaming. If an artist spends $10,000 making music to put on the platform, consider that it takes 229 streams to make one dollar.[9] This means that to recover the initial outlay, the music needs to be streamed 2,290,000 times.

As you can see from this example, there are important questions that need to be answered.

- The first: what is the artist trying to do?
- The second: is Spotify the best way to achieve it?

After asking pertinent questions, it may be the case that streaming is not the best way to get the desired result.

Red team blue team

Once a week, the Experts meet to discuss content ideas. During this meeting, a session called "Red Team, Blue Team" takes place. The name is borrowed from a term used in the military/ security, where roleplay is used to work through scenarios. The red team is the enemy and the blue team are defending.

---

[9] www.visualcapitalist.com

I first came across this concept in the brilliant TV show, *The News Room*, created by Aaron Sorkin, based around a fictitious cable news room.

In a couple of episodes, part of the news team secretly works on a special investigation. They are the red team. Once the red team feel the story is solid enough to break, they bring it to a meeting of the entire news team. Those not working on the story are the blue team. At this meeting it's the job of the red team to convince the blue team that the story is solid enough to air.

We use the same process with Experts. Content ideas are brought to the meeting and the person tabling the idea has to convince the rest of the editorial team that the idea is strong enough to spend time on. If the idea is a convincing proposition for the team, then the idea goes ahead. If not, the person pitching the idea does more work on it or scraps it.

As you can imagine, a lot of questions get asked. The main question is usually, "What are we trying to do?" This leads to the next question, "Is this the best way to do it?" Sometimes, the answer to the second question is no.

Once we know we've found the wrong way to do something, then we can start to think about the right way. We often arrive at the wrong way because we fail to ask the fundamental questions.

Avoiding difficult questions

Some people avoid asking questions because it can feel confrontational. It's easy to feel like a troublemaker if at every meeting you're questioning what's taking place.

Imagine someone has spent months preparing a presentation, thinking they've developed the perfect plan. Who wants to be the one to tell them it might need some more work, or worse, that they should go back to the drawing board and start again? Or, imagine you have a client who is about to hand you a large project. Isn't it better to shut up and take their money, rather than raise awkward questions?

In both cases, it's so tempting to take the line of least resistance, but that may be the wrong choice. Easy isn't always best.

Unless we challenge assumptions, the outcome could be a waste of time and money. Do we want to be the person who could have saved the project but instead settled for a quiet life?

Writing for the Harvard Business Review, Alison Wood Brooks and Leslie K. John say,

"Questioning is a uniquely powerful tool for unlocking value in organizations: It spurs learning and the exchange of ideas, it fuels innovation and performance improvement, it builds rapport and trust among team members. And it

can mitigate business risk by uncovering unforeseen pitfalls and hazards.

For some people, questioning comes easily. Their natural inquisitiveness, emotional intelligence, and ability to read people put the ideal question on the tip of their tongue. But most of us don't ask enough questions, nor do we pose our inquiries in an optimal way.

The good news is that by asking questions, we naturally improve our emotional intelligence, which in turn makes us better questioners–a virtuous cycle."[10]

It's easy to think of questions as obstacles in the road to getting somewhere fast. But what if you're moving fast towards the wrong destination, or you don't even know where you are supposed to be going?

Surely, it's better to determine the right destination, then find the best way to get there? Asking the right questions is vital.

FINAL QUESTION

Do you ask questions before starting a new project or just assume you have the answers?

---

[10] The Surprising Power of Questions, Harvard Business Review.

Treat Everything as a Pilot

QUICK TAKEAWAY
"Treat Everything as a pilot"
Don't be too keen to make your ideas permanent
from the outset. Test things and hold them lightly - it
makes it easier to drop them if they fail to work.

*"You don t learn to walk by following rules.
You learn by doing, and by falling over."*

Richard Branson

When I was young and trying to run a business, I
consumed many business and leadership books.

There was a recurring theme in most of them and that
was *vision*. I was encouraged to have a grand vision, a
master plan, to "set my face like flint" and not deviate
from the plan under any circumstances.

I've already discussed leadership here and stated that it
requires vision. How can you know if you are making
progress if you don't know your destination?

However, there is a danger that we can become so
obsessed with vision and strategy (both enormously
important) that we fail to be *flexible*. It is important to try
things and consider dropping them if they don't work.

My business successes are the things I tried that didn't fail. The list of things that didn't work is a long one, perhaps even longer than the list of things that did work!

The lesson here is that if we try to nail down everything from the outset, and only attempt the things we think will work, we may miss out on some opportunities.

The market research myth

If recent elections both in the UK and USA have proved anything, it's that you can't second guess the public. Pollsters and pundits will tell you how things will play out and then, boom! The result is entirely different.

In his book *Consumerolgy*, Philip Graves debunks what he calls "the market research myth" and the psychology of shopping.

"The fundamental tenet of market research is that you can ask people questions and that what they tell you in response will be true. And yet, as you will see, this is a largely baseless belief. In fact, it turns out that the opposite is far closer to the truth. When we ask people a question we make it very unlikely that they will tell us the truth; inviting a 'discussion' fares no better. The conscious mind finds it almost impossible to resist putting its spin on events. From the moment we do anything it introduces distortions; when the mind considers the future it does so with an idealism that is both optimistic and simultaneously devoid of any objective assessment of the past.

It's not the waste of money or the buck passing that I see as the biggest threat from this particular superstition. At stake is our ability to make good decisions. As someone once said, a mistake is only really a mistake if you don't learn from it. When market research is allowed into the decision-making process, and when that research is as flawed as social psychology and neuroscience are proving it to be, we lose the ability to learn from our mistakes. Research corrupts an organisation's learning process by inserting an erroneous fact - what people think - into the equation."[11]

I was one of those people who queued down the street outside the Apple Store for the first iPhone. I took the morning off work to do it. I remember my colleagues telling me I was mad and that there were better phones out there. The first iPhone lacked many of the features of its competitors, but that didn't matter. On paper, the first iPhone could have looked like a bad idea. Based purely on market research, it's likely it would have been rejected in its original incarnation.

Graves also cites these examples of failed market research:

"There are any number of accounts of where market research has been wrong. Products like Baileys liqueur that were rejected by consumers but launched anyway because of one senior manager's gut feel. Innovative concepts like the original Chrysler minivan and Compaq's PC network

---

[11] Philip Graves, Consumerology

servers, that were developed despite what consumers said because someone in the organization appreciated how they would change an aspect of people's lives. The research for a new mobile phone that concluded few customers would buy it, but it outsold the resulting estimates by a factor of ten. Advertising like the Heineken refreshes the parts... campaign that research respondents said they didn't like but, when someone convinced the company to use it in any case, went on to be massively successful. And opinion polls like the ones looking at what should happen to a portion of the BBC licence fee - one concluded that 66% of people supported the government's preferred option, another just 6%![12]

It's difficult to predict how an idea will work out. Some ideas we think won't work become a success and ones we would bet our house on fail miserably.

It's important to do your homework, to work out budgets, to analyse the size of a market, to carry out competitor analysis and do other due diligence to ask the right questions. But, there will be plenty of times in the life of your business when you have to just try something out and be open minded, so here's my advice:

Treat everything as a pilot.

---

[12] Philip Graves, Consumerology

The benefit of pilots

There are two benefits of using pilots. The first is to do with resistance to change.

I learnt this when I had the dubious pleasure of being on a church PCC (Parochial Church Council) for several years. If you've ever been on a church or local council committee then you'll know they can be the most depressing places on earth. Depending on the constitution of the group, getting anything done can be almost impossible. Resistance can be strong and often it's a battle of wills.

I recall being in meetings late into the night, where a section of the committee would dig their heels in and the chance of getting a positive vote was slim. Often this was simply down to their resistance to change.

This isn't just an issue on church or council committees, of course. You'll find this intransigence on the boards of FTSE100 companies and small businesses. For some, the biggest issue to fight is change!

I remember when my then boss took me to one side before a particularly crucial meeting. I think on this occasion it was to approve the employment of a new member of staff.

To be honest, the resistance to change was so common and deeply held, it could have been a debate on changing the brand of coffee. He turned to me shortly before the meeting and said, "It's a pilot!"

I was confused; this was the first time he had brought it up.

"A pilot?" I queried.

He smiled. "If we make this a pilot, then they'll know we're not asking them to do something permanent. They will be more likely to agree to it and, once it's done, they'll never scrap the idea."

It was a genius move.

We went into the meeting and proposed we run a pilot of employing a new team member, to see how it worked in practice. The motion was passed unanimously. As predicted, the new team member was a success and stayed for good.

After that meeting, we decided that every contentious issue would be put forward as a pilot!

You may be thinking this sounds like a dishonest approach. Not at all. The problem is that many people, when presented with a new idea, think you are setting it in stone; that it can't be undone if it goes wrong. Some things don't work out and anything can be undone, but you won't know until you've tried. By proposing a new idea as a pilot, everyone taking part in the decision can accept it. In effect, you are meeting them halfway.

We can't be certain anything will succeed. The trouble is, some people want that certainty and, without it, refuse to entertain change. A pilot breaks the deadlock.

No one is 100% right all the time

The most important reason for running a pilot is that no one can be 100% certain of success. We are all flawed and when we try to sell someone an idea, our reasoning can be wrapped up in our desire to make it happen. We can be so obsessed with success that rationality takes a back seat.

It's like falling in love. We are so determined to make it work that we overlook the things we don't want to see.

Since 2008, the Experts has tried out more ideas than I care to remember. Some of them were good, some bad, and some appropriate for a time, but we outgrew them or found a better way.

We sold software; we had a download site; we took donations; we sold subscriptions; we paywalled some content; we had multilingual versions of the site; we had multiple websites; we sold stuff on Amazon!

You would think that taking this approach might lead to people thinking we were flaky and easily changeable, but people have short memories. I can't remember half the stuff we tried in the past, so I doubt our readers can. All they care about is that we continue to develop the business to give them the best possible experience.

Better than yesterday

As mentioned earlier, when asked how we reached over 7 million readers, the simple answer was that I did whatever I could to ensure we had more readers today than yesterday. As long as that was happening, I knew we were growing.

This answer led to a second question: what do we actually *do* to make sure the numbers keep growing?

Are you ready for a deep, ground-breaking business strategy?

It's this... we do more of the stuff that works and less of the stuff that doesn't.

See, I told you it was genius.

Joking apart, it's so obvious it seems silly, but nevertheless it's an essential business strategy.

Hold on lightly

We need to hold onto everything lightly. If it's not working, then we drop it and move on. It's important not to get too attached to any part of a business, otherwise sentimentality takes over from rationality and we get attached to things that could waste a lot of time and money.

If you run a small business and wish it were bigger and better established, I want to let you in on a secret: you have a huge advantage over bigger, older businesses. You are agile and can change fast.

There is an equation I once heard about change that seems to hold true:

The speed of change is proportionate to the size and age of the organisation.

In other words, the bigger/older the organisation, the slower change can take place.

If you run a small, one-person business and you want to change your logo today, you can do it. Now imagine you are Ford Motor Co. Consider the layers of management that must be consulted. The design team must be involved, as well as the production team, who will need to change the logo on every part of each car made. Then there are mountains of documents and websites to update. Plus, there is the branding used on all the dealerships across the nation... all of that needs to change too.

The idea of treating everything as a pilot is much harder to apply for those larger, older entities - especially if they are manufacturing cars, toasters or washing machines.

The time and cost required to bring such products to market means it's hard to treat such changes as a pilot.

Over 5,000 failures

There are, however, some things even large well-established brands can do. James Dyson made several thousand versions of his now iconic Dyson vacuum cleaners, as Matthew Syed explains in his book *Black Box Thinking*:

"James Dyson worked through 5,126 failed prototypes for his dual cyclone vacuum before coming up with the design that made his fortune. These failures were essential to the pathway of learning. As Dyson put it: You can't develop new technology unless you test new ideas and learn when things go wrong. Failure is essential to invention."[13]

Be open to change

A few years ago, I received a call from a potential client who was developing some fantastic new technology for the professional audio industry. Chris is smart and has an excellent track record of creating ground-breaking technologies which are used by music and post professionals.

As is often the case, we had an initial call about his idea, then agreed to sign an NDA, so he and his partner Erik could talk with me in detail about this yet to be released product.

---

[13] Black Box Thinking, Matthew Syed

We spoke again a few days later, so he could pitch the product to me. It was, as I would expect from Chris, innovative and ground-breaking. He was using some clever ideas to replicate the behaviour of vintage and rare microphones that cost tens of thousands of pounds. The system was a combination of hardware and software and introduced a new workflow to the process of recording.

He asked my advice on how to proceed before he took it to market. The usual route for most companies working in the sector was to book a stand at NAMM, the leading industry trade show, then let people check it out. However, I still had reservations about the workflow. I was concerned that once the product had a public viewing, it would be much harder to take corrective action on any issues. Given that the brand hadn't even launched with this, their first product, I thought it a risky strategy.

I proposed an alternative option. My option was to rent an apartment near to the NAMM show and I would work with them to invite a select group of industry experts for private viewings. These would be made up of engineers and producers who work in top studios every day. If anyone could spot an issue it was these people.

What I didn't tell Chris and Erik at the time was that I was going to be sending some of the most difficult people I knew in the business! At least one of them could find a problem with *anything*. He could be a real pain in the butt, but I was interested to know his reaction.

The team went with the idea and set up a makeshift demo studio in a condo not far from the event. All of those we needed to come would be at the NAMM event anyway, so it suited everyone.

Over that week a steady stream of people went for their personal session with the team to check out the microphone. They could all see how much potential this mic modelling system had to offer. They also, as I hoped, gave their honest feedback.

While the feedback didn't take the product back to the drawing board, it did help inform changes that led to the final product, which we launched later that year.

The Townsend Sphere mic modelling system was launched on Indigogo on August 3, 2016. Our goal was to raise $40,000 in 30 days. By day two we had reached 200% of the target and by the end of the campaign the figure was $368,000. We had a winner!

It's good to have a vision; to know what you are trying to achieve. It would have been easy for Chris to think that the mic was finished and couldn't be improved. The Townsend team could have ignored the advice and pushed on regardless. They could have decided their idea was set in stone. Instead, they treated it with open hands, willing to learn and improve if necessary, and decided the final version could be better.

Today, the Townsend Sphere has won numerous awards, is in countless recording studios around the world and continues to outsell the supply they have.

Townsend Labs took advantage of their greatest strength: they are small and relatively young. To try and do what we did in a larger organisation would be hard, if not impossible.

I know people working in larger brands who are banging their heads against the wall as they try to implement change through many layers of management. If that were not bad enough, they also have to tip-toe though history and politics adopted over decades. As one person put it: it's the difference between turning a speed boat and an oil tanker.

When it comes to change, the adage "small is beautiful" is true, so embrace your flexibility.

Celebrate your size and age

Many of you reading this book will be a one-person operation, or may have two to three staff. If your organisation is small and young, then take advantage of it. Remain flexible and agile, treat ideas with a light touch and make changes if things aren't working.

No one wants to admit they are wrong. None of us want to abandon something we've put a great deal of effort into. No one wants to be seen to have made a mistake.

Those feelings are understandable.

However, to allow a moment of pride, embarrassment or just sheer bloody-mindedness keep you on a course that will end in failure is insanity.

Failures are not obstacles on the road to success, they are the steps we take to get there.

Hold things lightly and you'll have less chance of allowing your failures to prevent you from you making progress. Then you will reach goals you never thought possible.

FINAL QUESTION

Is there something in your business that isn't working that you need to stop doing?

Seven Dogs Chasing the Same Cat

QUICK TAKEAWAY
"Seven dogs chasing the same cat"
If you just do the same as everyone else, then you'll
be fighting for the same customers and that's
a much harder game.

*"Cherish forever what makes you unique,
'cuz you're really a yawn if it goes."*

Bette Midler

Would it surprise you to know that I was once a punk rocker? It was back in the original days of punk, when bands like the Sex Pistols, The Clash, and Stiff Little Fingers were hot property.

I was just a teenager living at home, so my parents were unimpressed by both my musical and fashion choices. I wore a pair of checked bondage trousers and Teddy Boy blue suede "brothel creepers". Safety pins and chains hung from various parts of me. I messed around with making my hair into a mohawk and dying it green or red.

When asked why I dressed this way, my answer was unintentionally hilarious: "I want to be different, like everybody else!"

What makes your business different? Have you even considered that question?

The only show in town

The world has shrunk considerably in the last 20 years. Potential customers now have limitless possibilities and business owners have considerable new challenges. One such challenge is that you are not the only gig in town.

One of my earliest jobs was working in a large music store in the centre of Birmingham in the UK. The store was called Jones and Crossland and was iconic in its day, with four departments - Guitars, Drums, Keyboards & Recording, and Orchestral instruments - spread over three large shop units, offering everything one could want for making music.

In the 1980s, if you wanted to buy the latest synth or guitar then the easiest way was to visit a store like this. Mail order was just starting up, but if you wanted something next-day then you could use a service run by the rail company Red Star Parcels. I always thought it sounded more like a socialist movement than a delivery brand.

Red Star was a ball ache. Once the customer had paid, the store had to go to the local rail station, fill in a pile of forms in triplicate and pay the cost of shipping. Then the item would be put on a train to the railway station nearest to the customer. When the parcel arrived at its destination, the customer would have to go to the station to pick it up, hoping that British Rail staff hadn't used it as a football during the journey. Few thought this was a good idea, especially if it was a £1,000 guitar or a £3,000 piece of studio equipment.

In the 80s, the internet wasn't even a twinkle in anyone's eye. If you wanted to buy something, you headed to your nearest dealer. If you wanted to read more about the product, you ordered the brochure by post. If your product developed a fault, you took it back to the store and the store sent it away to the manufacturer. Sometimes you would have to wait for weeks for it to come back repaired. If you were lucky, the dealer would lend you something else you could use in the meantime.

There may have been several dealerships in a larger city, but in most cities there was just one. In Birmingham, one of the largest cities in the UK, we had two main dealers, Jones and Crossland and Musical Exchanges.

In some cases, only one dealer would be allowed the rights to sell a certain brand, such as Tascam or Fostex. This was partly to reduce price wars and, more often than not, because there wasn't enough supply to meet demand.

I recall on many occasions waiting for large trucks to pull up outside the Keyboard and Synth department where I worked, wondering if it was the stock we were desperate for. Some days an entire truck would deliver stock from just one brand, like Roland, and we would find ourselves knee deep in Juno 60s, Jupiter 8s and TR909 drum machines. It would take hours to book it all into stock, carefully logging each serial number. Then we would go through a book of customer back orders. No sooner had the stock arrived, it went out to new customers who had patiently waited, often weeks, sometimes even months.

For many living in smaller parts of the UK, their town wasn't big enough to sustain a music store. Some of those customers travelled for miles to try out gear and order it, to then go home and wait until they could return to pick up their musical equipment.

What I've described so far is the product side of commerce a few decades ago. It was no different for services. In the city of Birmingham, I believe there were less than three professional recording studios. One of the most popular was called Rich Bitch. It hosted both rehearsal rooms and a 32-track digital studio built around a Mitsubishi digital recorder.

Studios weren't unique in their scarcity. Outside the world of recording services, if you wanted a plumber, painter or mechanic, you would have to leaf through the phone book or its trade version, *The Yellow Pages*, or ask a friend if they knew of anyone. Most towns had just one or two tradespeople in each trade.

Getting a trade could take days or weeks. If they were popular and busy, it could take months! If you wanted to know whether you could trust them, you needed to ask a friend or one of their existing customers. There were no review websites.

Finally, paying for things was not straightforward either. You could pay using cash, cheque or, for large amounts, by banker's draft. Cheques would need to clear the bank before the goods were released or the job was started. In some cases, you could also use credit cards, but not via lightweight plastic Bluetooth powered devices. These were these large, metal, clunky machines that would imprint details on a voucher, the information produced in triplicate. You would need to sign the form and the seller would then have to phone the credit card company and speak to a real person to see if you had the money, and to check the card hadn't been stolen. Once this process was complete, there would be the slide and "clunk, clunk" of the credit card machine and the transaction was complete.

What I've described sounds like an ordeal compared to modern commerce. It might have been, but nobody knew any different - it was life!

There's always someone else

Now you can find a product or service in seconds via a web search. There won't be one dealer but hundreds offering the same product or service.

You can check out the prices and compare them. You can also see what the seller's reputation is like, with a multitude of online reviews, real or otherwise.

You don't need a brochure, because there will be an image and/or video online, rich with information for you to check out. If you want to know what "real people" think of the product, then you'll find both specialist websites (like the Experts) plus hundreds of online YouTube reviews, many made just hours after the product was released. (It seems every person and their dog is making YouTube reviews these days).

With modern shipping methods, and depending on where you live, a product can be with you in a couple of days, or even hours in larger cities. If you are buying software, then it is with you in a few minutes.

If you don't like what you have bought, or you've changed your mind, then you can ship it back, often at no cost to you, and have the money back in your account in days.

Speaking of money, there's a multitude of ways to pay, cash being the least used. There are debit and credit cards, interest free payment schemes like Klarna, Paypal, Apple Pay and online credit with instant decisions.

Modern commerce is a buyer's dream.

However, the things that have made things better for the buyer present a whole new set of challenges for those trying to sell their product or service. The greatest of these is *ubiquity.*

If someone doesn't like your product, service, price or shipping time, or has watched a poor YouTube review, or worse, read a vindictive angry review, they can go and buy it somewhere else. With the rise of online forums and social media it's possible for one person to trash your reputation in a matter of hours. Even if the complaint is untrue, by the time you've had chance to repair it, the damage may already be done.

Even if you work in the business to business (B2B) world, the challenges are the same. Where there were once a few people in your profession, now with the internet your clients have the potential to use anyone, anywhere. In fact, 90% of Sociatech's clients are not in the UK - they are based in the USA, Germany, Israel, Canada and other places across the globe.

Where once it was IBM, British Airways or McDonalds who were global, now every business can be global - in many cases, having a worldwide reach from a bedroom or a shed in the garden.

When I set up the blog back in 2008, it was a very new thing. At that point, most of the information available in the industry was print based. Web-based content publishing was in its infancy. Few published video-based reviews and tutorials, and YouTube was relatively small compared to the reach it has today. Back then, YouTube videos were in SD quality. Social media was in its early stages and not seen as a significant way to build a business.

Fast forward to today and every man, woman, and child is a blogger, influencer or YouTube sensation.

In the music technology industry, as soon as a product is released you can find half a dozen "reviews" for it. A large number of the public don't care who makes these videos, and there seems to be some confusion or apathy around the whole concept of authority.

As has sadly become clear during the Covid19 global pandemic that began in 2020, now everyone is a scientist, a virologist or an epidemiologist. All they need is an internet connection!

So, how does one survive in this kind of climate? How does a business stay ahead and avoid becoming just another business doing the same thing?

Difference matters

I was in a meeting with the Experts management team one day and there was a discussion around the issue of ubiquity. A product would be released and there would be a hundred stories in a matter of days on various websites. There would be hundreds of reviews posted on YouTube of varying quality. It seemed the music technology industry was becoming saturated with the same data. It was, as I suggested, "Seven dogs chasing the same cat."

What do I mean by this? The more dogs are in the race, the less chance there is of any of them winning. The best-case scenario is that one dog wins. How do we deal with that?

The answer is, you stop chasing the cats they are chasing. You change the game and find a point of difference.

So, the Experts made some choices. We would stop doing some of the things everyone else was doing and concentrate on what we did best. Let those who are good at some things have those things and let those who are fighting over the same stuff battle it out between themselves.

For example, in the music technology industry, few do product reviews better than *Sound on Sound*. The quality and depth of their work is second to none. I've known Paul White from *Sound on Sound* for over 35 years and have known the current editor, Sam Inglis, for several years too. I count them as friends in the industry who have worked hard to make *Sound on Sound* the high-quality publication it is. So, I'm happy to recommend them as the best place to read product reviews. I still read them and have for years.

A few weeks ago, Sam called me to discuss a product review that both *Sound on Sound* and the Experts were conducting. We wanted to make sure we weren't stepping on each other's toes and ensure the readership of both publications got a unique perspective from each.

It is because of excellent publications like *Sound on Sound,* and the tsunami of online reviews, that the Experts reduced their reviews output, choosing to test a much smaller set of products. You might think that's unwise - aren't reviews popular? Yes, they are, but if there are hundreds of people fighting for a slice of the pie then, even if you get a slice, it's a lot smaller.

In such a scenario, you have to assess if battling it out is the best use of your resources. I happen to think it's better to concentrate on the things that you can do better; the things that others are ignoring.

You can either be the best or do something different. The last thing you should do is chase the same cat.

Part of our business strategy is simple: look at what everyone else is doing and do something else. If you can't win the game, then change it.

Some of you might be reading this now thinking, hasn't he just given away the secret of the Experts success? Well, yes and no. I've given the basic outline of the strategy, but I'm not dumb enough to say what choices we make to respond to an overcrowded market.

Am I concerned others will try to copy the model? Some will, but they will need to do it better. If they do, then it might be time for us to do something different again.

Be courageous

I'd also like to suggest that it takes courage to diverge from the crowd. I recall calling a friend a few months ago who was "chasing the same cat" and told him how he could do something different. He completely ignored me and just followed the crowd, chasing the same cat. As my Dad said, "I can't put my head on their shoulders."

It takes courage to do things differently.

One of my business heroes is Steve Jobs, CEO of Apple for many years before his untimely death in 2011. Apple were the brand who coined the phrase "Think Different", which led to the renaissance of a brand that had been languishing.

Apple were the first brand to remove floppy discs from computers, and remove DVD drives, and remove fixed network connections. Apple decided to ditch Adobe Flash, the most ubiquitous web technology at the time. Many observers thought they were mad, because every other computer had these technologies. But Apple thought differently.

As we all now know, the entire industry ended up following Apple's lead and continues to do so.

Apple don't chase the same cat and that's the reason people are willing to pay a premium for their products.

Some see Apple's walled garden approach to the design of both hardware and software as a weakness that limits their appeal, but sales figures tell a different story. Apple is one of the richest companies on the planet, with a larger income than the GDP of some smaller countries.

Ubiquity threatens price

If your products or services are the same as everyone else's, then you immediately enter a price sensitive market. If you are the only one doing what you do then, within reason, you can determine the price.

I'll repeat this:

To succeed in business, you either have to be better or different.

Take the ingenious products from the wonderful team at Sound Radix, who I'm glad to have as clients and friends. They make truly unique software products for the audio industry. Their team has some of the smartest software developers on the planet.

Even smarter, they are not making the same software as other developers. In the audio world there's a trend to try and make software emulations of older audio hardware. In some cases, there are 30 or 40 versions of the same product, some of which are free. You have to either be truly brave or insanely stupid to try to get rich doing that!

If you run a service business, then consider this:

- What skill do you have that is in short supply?
- What do you excel at? If you are not sure, this is what your clients say you are good at and the reason why they recommend you to others
- Is there a gap in the market that others are missing? (Take care when considering this question. Sometimes there's a gap because there isn't a demand in the first place)

Marketing empathy

The best sellers think like buyers. It's what we call at Sociatech, "marketing empathy". The dictionary defines empathy as the ability to understand and share the feelings of another.

In order to sell effectively, you need to know how your potential buyers feel about things. What makes them happy? What impresses them? What matters most to them? What problems do they need to overcome?

All this market intelligence will help you to find your niche.

The best thing since sliced bread

We used to live in Greenwich in London. It is a pretty part of the UK capital, with tightly knit streets of Victorian terraces, townhouses and a couple of rows of specialist shops like a butcher, greengrocer, cheese and bread shop, and fish monger. Then there is the centre of Greenwich, with lots of restaurants, coffee shops and cafés. It also has two supermarkets: a Sainsbury and Co-Op Local, so we were just a couple of minutes' walk away from supplies.

Every Saturday morning, a queue would form up the street, where the row of specialist shops was located. Sometimes it would take 15 minutes to get into the store. If you were early enough, you would get what you were queuing for, but often not.

We were queuing for bread. Not just any bread, but bread costing £3 a loaf! Just one minute away there was no queue for bread costing 50p a loaf.

The bread in the supermarket was piled high and perhaps OK for toast and sandwiches, but the sourdough bread we queued for on a Saturday morning was sublime.

Both the stuff in the supermarkets and at the bakers was *bread*, but one of these establishments had a queue of people down the street who were willing to pay a premium. You might think the people willing to wait and pay through the nose were insane, but that's irrelevant. What matters is that some people valued the quality enough to do so.

The more unique you are, the less you'll be fighting for the same customers, and the less price sensitive your potential customers will be. People are willing to pay a premium if the product is exclusive. They are also willing to pay a premium if your product and service is better.

Price is a message

Furthermore, price is a *message*. It defines the type of customer you are likely to get. Some brands intentionally price their products to exclude certain people from buying them.

There's nothing that amuses me more than seeing a comment on social media saying, "If you priced it lower, then you would sell more." My first reaction is to say, "No shit, Sherlock." However, I usually observe that the product has been priced intentionally to attract a certain customer. They are not trying to get *more* customers, they are trying to get *better* ones.

If you are dreaming of buying a £70,000 Ferrari but gulping when you see the price of a set of new tyres or a service, then it's not for you. A Ferrari is aimed at people who don't even think about those things. As my Dad used to say, "If you can't afford the tyres, you can't afford the car."

We are now moving into the area of product positioning and target markets. We won't go in-depth, but suffice to say, you need to clearly define *what* you are selling and *who* you are selling it to.

Who are your customers?

If your answer is that you are "targeting everyone" you need to think again. That's not a target, it's a "throw enough mud and some will stick" approach and it doesn't work. You'll end up trying to meet everyone's needs and meeting no one's.

You wouldn't join a dating website and say you were looking for anyone, who likes anything, who doesn't care who they meet. That would be insane.

Your customer targeting is exactly the same. Define what you are offering and who it is for. The clearer you are about your offer and the customer, the easier it will be to target and win them.

We live in a world where it's possible to buy a Chinese drum from a woman who lives in a wood in the middle of France. It's possible to be niche, so take advantage of it!

The more you generalise, the greater the competition. The more you specialise, the smaller the competition.

Don't be one of the seven dogs chasing the same cat; you have less chance of winning.

The smart people find a new cat, then build such an attractive business that the cat ends up chasing them!

FINAL QUESTION

What makes you unique?

Do the Right Thing
Whatever the Cost

QUICK TAKEAWAY
"Do the right thing whatever the cost"
There are times when you are tempted to take
shortcuts in business. Never compromise your values,
even if it costs money to do the right thing.

*"Image is what people think we are.
Integrity is what we really are."*
John C. Maxwell

In the lifetime of the Expert websites, the following
scenario has happened several times. I get one of those
calls. It's usually Mike, my co-Director, calling to say,
"Russ, we have to take that article down."

Then follows a discussion about why we should. It's
usually a brand who is unhappy about something we've
published about their product or their policy. At some
point, we will discuss the legal issues: is it libellous or just
uncomfortable for the brand who are complaining?

One such occasion was when the blog had run a contest
on behalf of a brand and they had not followed through
with delivering the prizes. I'm not talking days or weeks;
months had passed.

The winners were getting fed up, wondering if they were ever going to see their prizes, and who could blame them? I was wondering the same thing. Eric, our Community Manager at the time, asked me what to do. He had exhausted every possible avenue with all our contacts at the brand and was at a loss as to how to resolve the situation. The delays were starting to damage our brand reputation. It was possible that people were starting to think the contest was a scam.

I emailed Eric and told him to give the winners the email address of the CEO of the brand.

"Are you sure?" he queried.

"Yes, we've been given no choice and we've run out of options," I told him.

Within five minutes of me telling him to do that, my phone was ringing. It was my PR contact at the brand. I knew why he was calling.

"Russ," said the voice at the end of the phone. "Our CEO is pissed at you. He has emails from people asking where their prizes are."

The person calling me was a good friend, and we had spoken several times about the issue.

"So, where are the prizes?" I asked.

"He's looking into it now. It should be sorted today, but he's not happy," he replied.

"I'm sure he's not, Mark, but it was the only option left and if this was happening in my company, I would like to know."

He agreed. The call wasn't really for Mark to shout at me. It was so he could tell his boss that he had!

Within days, the winners got their prizes. We didn't get a card from the CEO that Christmas. A year later he was gone, although I don't think it had anything to do with prizes.

It might seem like a tiny issue for a large, multi-million-dollar brand - one that wouldn't even move the needle - but following through on your promises is essential if you want people to trust you.

Take it down!

A couple of years later, Mike was on the phone with me again. Same brand, different CEO.

"Russ, we've been told to pull down the story on their new plan," he said.

"But it's a stupid idea and doesn't benefit their users," I replied.

"I know," said Mike. "But it's the CEO's personal project and if we don't pull it then he's cutting us off."

"What does that mean?" I asked.

"It means they will cancel all ad spend with us for a start," he continued. "They also plan to cut us out of all press releases in the future. He is really angry!"

I thought for a second.

"Did we say anything untrue?"

"Not at all," Mike replied. "What we said is the truth. It's a dumb idea and not something we would recommend to our readers."

"What's the ad spend?" I asked.

"Over $20,000 per year," replied Mike.

"OK, are we agreed that we stand our ground on this one?" I asked.

Mike was in agreement with me. In all the years I've known him, I've never seen Mike compromise on integrity.

In the proceeding weeks the brand followed through on their threats. Their advertising spend was cancelled and we got stonewalled by their PR team. Although, the PR team weren't as smart as they thought. We'd cultivated such a strong relationship with other people who worked at the brand that we continued to get the information we needed to be able to inform our readers of new products and other pertinent news. Mike and I knew that from the start - the only damage they could inflict on us was financial.

So why did we take a stand, knowing that revenue would be lost?

What price trust?

It's simple. Our readers trust us to tell the truth. *They* are our audience, not the brands. The minute we lose their trust, it's game over. Working with brands who pay for advertising and, at the same time, offering an impartial view to our community is a hard enough balancing act. This is why, for us, compromise is not an option.

The end of the story is that the boss left. The idea we thought was bad for users went away and, with a new boss, the relationship was restored. Now it's better than ever.

This wasn't a case of wanting to be right; it was a case of doing the right thing.

Now it's our turn

Fast forward to a few years later. Each year, the Experts runs an end of year prize draw, consisting of around 30 prizes generously donated by many of our partners. The prize draw was run and the winners selected. Now it was time to get the prizes to them in various parts of the world.

It seems that history has a funny way of repeating itself and, indeed, of testing us.

I got a call from one of the Experts team.

"Russ, we've got a problem with one of the prizes," they said. "It seems we forgot to ask the brand before we offered one of their products as a prize."

For me the answer was simple.

"Give me an hour," I said. "Let me talk to the CEO of the brand."

As soon as I was off the phone, I emailed the CEO, a good friend and someone I have a lot of time for. I explained what had happened and he could see the fix we were in.

It wasn't his fault though, it was ours, so why should he take either the financial or reputational hit for our mistake?

"How much?" I asked him, and he told me.

"Send me an invoice and I'll pay it right away," I said.

For me it was a no-brainer. I couldn't, on one hand, blast the CEO of a company for not following through on his prize, but ignore the problem my own company had created. That would be hypocrisy. Furthermore, the winner was expecting the prize and it wasn't his fault our team hadn't got their act together.

Decisions, decisions

Various sources suggest the average human makes approximately 35,000 decisions each day. Researchers at Cornell estimate we make over 220 choices about what food to eat each day.[14]

In business we make thousands of decisions each day. Should I read this email now or later? Pay this bill now or tomorrow? Buy this software or that software?

Many of the decisions we make have a relatively low impact on the long term good of our business, but some decisions have huge ramifications.

Here's a simple value to hold to. In fact, it's my number one business value...

Do the right thing, whatever the cost.

As the earlier stories have shown, doing the right thing may cost us tens of thousands of pounds, or at other times just a few hundred. But the amount is irrelevant.

---

[14] Mindless Eating: The 200 Daily Food Decisions We Overlook

Make me an offer

Whenever someone accuses the Experts of writing positive content for a brand, suggesting they've, "paid you to say nice things about them", I have one response:

"Make me an offer!"

What I mean is, the person is suggesting that our integrity can be bought. If that's true, then there must be an amount of money we would take to compromise our integrity. So, go on, make us an offer!

To date no one has taken me up on the challenge. I'm glad for them. I know they don't have enough money. If there *was* a number, then our integrity would be a sham.

This is a value our entire team knows. It means that when it comes to making decisions, it's a much simpler choice.

What should I do?

I recall being on a team call a few years ago and one of the contributors who was writing a review asked a question.

"I've got this product to review and I don't think it's very good," he said. "What should I do?"

"What's our top value?" I asked.

Someone replied, "Do the right thing whatever the cost."

Then a discussion ensued about what we should do. By the end of the debate, we decided it would be best for him to go back to the brand, tell them his concerns about the product, and let them decide what we should do. They decided to postpone the review, make the changes we were suggesting to improve the product, and *then* have us review it.

In his article "Doing the Right Thing" written for the Institute for Ethical Leadership, Desmond Berghofer says,

"If a person comes to a position of power as a leader in an organization or in society without knowing how to do the right thing, then the people under his or her influence are in for a bad time. At worst they will find themselves plunged into brutal conflict with outside forces, or at best they will spend a lot of time and energy struggling with internal disharmony and damage control."[15]

It is essential to have an uncompromising set of values at the heart of your business. Without them, your business reputation will suffer and in the long term it could be damaged irreparably.

---

[15] Doing the Right Thing by Desmond Berghofer

The errors of youth

In my younger years, I allowed myself to be compromised. If I forgot to do something, I would lie to try and cover up. I'd let people down and then make some excuse, or blame someone else. I'm ashamed by the lack of integrity I showed for many years, thinking it was the easy way to avoid my own shortcomings.

As I said earlier, I've always found this quote on wisdom helpful. "Wisdom is doing the right thing, and we know how to do the right thing because we've done the wrong thing before."

Compromise has a way of catching up with you and over time people stop trusting you. That's what happened to me. I'd be passed over for promotion; I was a flake who couldn't be trusted. Or, I was not asked to do the important client work. After all, who was going to risk their best client on someone like me? The only person I was fooling was myself. People knew when I was lying to cover up my mistakes.

A lifetime lesson

The reality is, I remain flawed, tempted and open to compromise. Upholding one's integrity isn't a once in a lifetime decision, then you're fixed.

I know some leaders who I thought were one step away from being sainted, who then lost it all.

Don't read this and think I'm a saint, far from it. I still say and do some dumb things. I make the wrong choices. However, I know the standard I am supposed to live to and when I have fallen short.

This is a daily journey, when presented with new decisions both large and small. I'm only as good as my last decision and so I must take careful steps to avoid making the wrong one. I'm only one bad decision away from blowing it.

You may be a one-person operation or running a multi-billion-dollar company. The size is irrelevant, because doing the right thing is always the right thing to do. At times it's going to cost you money, but consider the alternative: not doing the right thing could cost you everything.

FINAL QUESTION

Are you making compromises that could
be affecting your reputation?

Don't Blame Them, Train Them

QUICK TAKEAWAY
"Don't blame them, train them"
It's easy to jump to blame people when things go wrong in your business. What matters more is helping the person (and ultimately your business) to grow.

"People who blame things rarely change things. Blame is an unassailable change-avoidance strategy."

Andy Stanley

There are few things more worrying than being on an airplane when a problem occurs. I do more than the average amount of flying for my work, and my family live in a different part of the country to me, so I've built up my air miles over the years.

It was just before Christmas, December 2019, and I was making my way home after seeing Mum and Dad. News had come in that there were storms at home and the flight may be cancelled. It wasn't, which in hindsight was a bad idea.

We were flying in a twin turbo prop - much smaller than the average 737 jet - so it's much easier to feel the bumps during flight.

As we made the final descent into Belfast City airport, flying over Belfast Lough, we bumped hard as the wind and rain battered the plane. In this kind of weather, our plane was bouncing in every direction as the wind gusted.

I'd experienced this landing many times, so I was aware of what landmarks to look out for as we came in.

The turn over my home, Bangor, for the final descent... tick.

The Culloden Estate hotel... tick. We were getting closer.

Holywood town... tick.

B&Q and IKEA... tick.

We were seconds away from landing and just as the wheels were about to touch the tarmac, suddenly the engines roared and the plane pulled up hard into the clouds again.

Those few seconds seemed to last a lifetime. Everything I expected to happen didn't. We hadn't made it down and we were flying away again. No one on the plane spoke and the Captain said nothing for what seemed like an age. Then, over the tannoy, we were told that we were going around again to try another landing. As you can imagine, the plane was silent as the crew tried to land again. This time, after a few minutes of palpable fear, we were on the ground.

Apparently, we were not in that much danger and this is a common occurrence when flying in windy conditions, but it was an experience I wouldn't want to have again.

Flying is one of the safest forms of travel, if not *the* safest on the planet. Because of the sensational headlines produced when a plane crashes, we are led to believe that it's not. The data tells me I was more likely to die in the cab home from the airport; my irrational feelings told me otherwise.

Mistakes happen, that's not the issue

In his book *Black Box Thinking*, Matthew Syed draws a comparison between the safety record of the airline industry and that of the medical profession. The aim of the book is to help those in leadership to learn from their mistakes.

The title alludes to how the airline industry and the medical industry deal with failure. One would think that a hospital is a safe place - much safer than travelling on an airplane. However, the data shows a stark picture.

"According to the Journal of Patient Safety, 400,000 people die every year in American hospitals alone due to preventable error. That is like two jumbo jets crashing every day or 9/11 happening every few days. In the UK, too, the

numbers are shocking. Until healthcare learns to respond positively to failure, things will not improve. "[16]

Syed looks at how the airline industry responds to a plane crash, as well as incidents where the plane didn't crash, but issues could have led to catastrophic results.

The airline industry is safe because they work to find out what happens during these rare incidents, rather than trying to apportion blame. Syed thinks the medical profession has much to learn from this approach.

"How the f**k could this happen?"

It was a few months after a new member of the Expert team had arrived. A hugely capable person, with skills in management and data analysis, he had been given a large brand to handle. The account was worth tens of thousands of pounds; you can count those clients on one hand.

Our main contact at the brand (thankfully, a good friend) was asking us to send over a summary of the work they had been paying for during the billing period. The contract included lots of small pieces of content over an extended period of time which, when added up, represented a significant amount of work.

As we began to compile the list of the work completed, something didn't look right. We couldn't find the

---

[16] Black Box Thinking, Mathew Syed

content. It was at this point that I received a call to alert me of the anomaly. Even though I'm a creative type and very visceral in my approach, I've learnt over the years that data is my friend. Much of my work these day as CEO of the Experts is looking at data and using it to inform decision making. I used to ignore it, but now I do so at my peril.

I knew the only way to get to the bottom of the issue was to conduct a full audit of the account and the work done. I asked for it to be on my desk the same day. Later that day, the audit arrived and it didn't look good. We couldn't find the content because it hadn't been done.

My first thought was, "How the f**k could this happen?"

When a problem happens in business you have to deal with both the facts and the feelings. My feelings told me I wanted to shout and scream. Thankfully, my head told me that while it'd make me feel better for a short while, that wouldn't help.

When it comes to situations like this, the first thing I do is call Mike, my co-Director. There are a number of reasons. The first is that I know I can be real with him and scream and swear. This helps cool down the reactor. Secondly, Mike has as much skin in the game as me. We share this business; he has as much to win or lose, so he knows how I'm feeling. Thirdly, while Mike may have the same vision as me, he is nothing like me when it comes to these issues. I'm more likely to use my heart, he his head.

We spoke at length about the gravity of the situation. Mike agreed to email the client and explain our findings and also what we proposed to do about it. Lesson one, when you screw up, put your hands up and do whatever it takes to put it right. This solved the external issues.

Opening the black box

However, of equal importance was to discover how this happened and how we could prevent it happening again. We needed to examine the black box.

Although it might seem natural to want to find someone to blame, I knew it would do little to fix the reason the problem had happened.

The team member responsible for the account was falling over himself to apologise, so I knew he took the matter seriously.

The next task was to find out how it had happened. Was it carelessness or some larger systemic failure? Sometimes planes crash because of a catastrophic fault, but it can also be pilot error. Knowing which it is can save lives in future, hence the reason the airline industry takes accidents so seriously.

What would happen when we opened our black box?

As we looked into the matter, we found it was due to a number of factors. There were both people and system failures. What became clear was that it wasn't the new team member's fault. We needed to fix certain systems and show him how to use them effectively.

Don't blame them, train them!

"A great leader will always take ownership of the results. They won't try to find excuses or blame others, because when you place blame elsewhere, you're ultimately pulling on the handbrake for any kind of improvement."[17]

The outcome of that episode was sobering, but we turned a mess into a learning experience for both the company and the individual concerned.

The business shortcomings cost us in the short term, but I believe our approach to dealing with them will make us a better business.

Once we had discovered the issues we went back to the client and explained what had happened and what we planned to do to remedy the situation. We gave them a number of options to choose from, including putting the matter right and also compensation.

You may be wondering how it felt to be the person on the other end of this experience, so I asked the staff member to write his thoughts and express how it felt to be in the

---

[17] Gordon Tredgold, Inc

eye of the storm; whether we handled the situation well and helped him in his role.

"Whether it is being overwhelmed in a new role, having a moment of carelessness, or making a seemingly simple oversight, mistakes happen - even to the most conscientious of us. After a mistake, it can feel like you are stuck in a kind of limbo. Am I going to get fired? Will I lose this contract? Have I ruined my reputation? Every little detail feels magnified and you get swept under a tidal wave of stress and anxiety.

Making this mistake forced me to reset. A hard stop! But the support I received helped ease the stress and anxiety. There was no blame culture here. Time was taken to identify the issues that preceded the error, to help us all understand why it had happened.

Most crucially, it allowed us, as a team, to put the correct processes in place to ensure it never happened again. The guidance and mentorship I received during all this meant that I learned and I grew (a hell of a lot). But I also felt overwhelmingly valued; still trusted to continue to produce results in my role.

This experience is why the value 'Don't Blame Them, Train Them' will stick with me throughout my career."

The blame game

We live in a world where business leaders are so concerned by the culture of blame and the possibility of litigation, that many now avoid admitting they got things wrong.

Mistakes are inevitable. There isn't a business on the planet that doesn't have issues lurking around until one day they blow up. If we simply look for blame in those situations, we miss the chance of building a better business.

FINAL QUESTION

Do you blame others when things go wrong or do you try to discover how to ensure the problem gets fixed?

Profit is What You Don't Spend

QUICK TAKEAWAY
"Profit is what you don't spend"
Do everything you can to reduce costs.
The less money you spend trying to make it,
the more you'll have left over.

"I've got the brains, you've got the looks
Let's make lots of money."
Pet Shop Boys

One of the most interesting discoveries I've made working in the creative industry is how many people unintentionally began their business. I speak with many professional musicians, producers, mixers and engineers and if you ask, they'll tell you there was no master plan to own a business. In most cases, it was the last thing on their mind.

Accidental business owners

One minute they are mixing some tracks or recording a band, and a decade later they wake up and find they are running a business. What began as one-person venture grew organically and now they have premises and, in some cases, employ staff. Now there are taxes to think about, insurance, healthcare, pensions, legal matters... the list goes on.

I call these people "accidental business owners". I mean no disrespect. In fact, when I say it to people who are calling me for advice, they agree entirely. "I didn't get into this to run a business," they often say, as they look around the building they rent with ten staff.

Given that background, when you start to talk about profit, you can be met with a blank expression. This is when you realise that although the person is now running a business, profit is an afterthought, not an intentional plan.

People are confused when it comes to profit. I'm not surprised. If you check out some of the definitions for profit, it is certainly confusing.

What is profit?

Investopedia defines it this way,

"Profit describes the financial benefit realised when revenue generated from a business activity exceeds the expenses, costs, and taxes involved in sustaining the activity in question. Any profits earned funnel back to business owners, who choose to either pocket the cash or reinvest it back into the business. Profit is calculated as total revenue less total expenses."[18]

Collins Dictionary says,

---

[18] www.investopedia.com

"A profit is an amount of money that you gain when you are paid more for something than it cost you to make, get, or do it."[19]

And Wikipedia:

"Profit, in accounting, is an income distributed to the owner in a profitable market production process (business). Profit is a measure of profitability which is the owner's major interest in the income-formation process of market production." [20]

Profit is something every business needs to think about. It can be the difference between success and failure. If we ignore it, we could be working 18 hours, 7 days a week and losing money. Yes, that's right, you can be turning over lots of money and losing it at the same time. It's what is commonly known as a "busy fool".

The aim of every business is to generate as much money as possible while minimising cost.

The turnover trap

I needed to apply for a mortgage a couple of years ago and as I'm self-employed, the bank wanted to see several years of accounts. A couple of days later I found myself on the phone with someone from the bank who was

---

[19] Collins Dictionary
[20] Wikipedia

asking me to explain the significant drop in turnover in one of my businesses during a particular year.

The reason was that I'd moved some operations from one business to the other. The account for the other business reflected this, but the bank was having none of it. As far as the bank were concerned, it was all about turnover.

However, turnover is not the most important number to look at. Profit is what matters. Let me illustrate with this example:

Let's say I have a business that turns over £100,000 a year and, after costs, it makes £30,000 profit. I need to draw £50,000 to cover my living expenses, so I'm £20,000 short.

Next year, the accounts show that the turnover has dropped to £60,000. That looks worse. But, drilling down into the accounts, they show that the business made a £55,000 profit - more than enough to cover my living expenses.

How is this possible? Let's take a closer look at the business.

It's a service business and everyone works from home, so there are only a few overheads related to business activity. Overheads are fixed costs that don't change, irrespective of how much turnover occurs.

In the example above, during the first year there were two additional team members who cost the business £65,000. The remaining £5,000 was spent on things like phones and other minor costs.

In the second year, the two additional team members no longer worked for the business, so that cost was gone, but of course the turnover had decreased too. However, even though the business turnover dropped by 40%, the profit had doubled. In this new scenario, I could afford to pay myself enough to cover my personal needs and leave £5,000 in the business.

This is possible when you reduce costs, because what's left is profit.

Profit is what you don't spend.

This is a greatly simplified example and doesn't take into account things like tax, but I hope you get the point.

It's easy to look at the top number of turnover and think a business is doing well, but ignore the important number, which is profit. There's an old business mantra: "turnover is vanity, but profit is sanity".

I'm a stickler for keeping down costs. I do everything I can to avoid spending money in the business. That means taking care of every little detail.

If one of my team comes to ask whether we can invest in something, they have to make a strong case. I had someone working for me who would be on the phone every month suggesting we start using a piece of software, or we buy an item for the business. I recall one of those calls where I asked him to justify why we should do it. He made a vague case of needing a subscription for a software package for the team. It was something like £30 per team member per month, and we had five in the team at the time. Do the math, that's £150 per month, or an annual bill of £1,800.

At this point I'm thinking about how much more work we'll need to do to generate that £1,800. If, for example, we make a 50% margin on all work, we would need to generate £3,600 additional income to break even on the investment.

I was unconvinced so I said to him, "You know profit is what we don't spend?"

He was taken aback and said, "Well that's not true." He went on to quote me one of the many business school definitions of profit. He didn't get it.

I was trying to explain to him that if we invest in something, it has to pay for itself many times over to be worth it. Was this new software really going to add value to the business, or would it just be nice to have? Could we do the job without it? Which leads me to my second point...

Whose money are you spending?

Was this person spending the business' money as if it was his own?

When I work with client budgets, be it for an advertising campaign, a recording session, or a film shoot for an advert, I spend it like it's my money - and I expect my teams to spend my money like it's *their* money.

You'd be amazed how people will spend money differently when it's *theirs* as opposed to their employer's. I happen to think we should have the same attitude to spending, irrespective of whose money it is.

A stakeholder mentality

There's a word for this: it's called being a *stakeholder*.

A friend of mine once asked me the question: *Why is there always popcorn all over the floor of a movie theatre at the end of a show?*

The answer is simple: the people who do that don't own the movie theatre.

I find that a powerful illustration of what a stakeholder is - and I don't mean it in the conventional sense of the word.

A stakeholder is someone who treats the business as if it's *their* business, irrespective of who owns it.

Stakeholders are the best kind of people to have on your team. They treat your customers as if they were their customers and your money as if it was their money.

Even if you don't have staff and you generally hire freelancers for your projects, make sure they have the attitude of a stakeholder.

This week I had a call with one of my team who runs the department which looks after partnerships at Production Expert. To improve communication with our clients, he is setting up a CRM system. I asked him for his recommendation on the right software to do this. He talked me through the options and at the end of it he said, "I've done the research and on balance, this is the system we should use, because right now it's free and if we grow, we can pay to bolt on more options."

I knew at the end of that call that he was making the decision as if it was his business. Not because he had chosen the free option, but because he had considered a number of options and decided that even though we could spend money and get lots of features, the system he'd picked was free and could grow with us. He's a stakeholder; he is treating the business as if it's his.

Last Christmas, we gave that member of the team an unexpected bonus of several thousand pounds, paid for by a significant revenue boost he played a part in. After all, if he's treating the business like it's his, then he should be rewarded as if it's his too.

Every decision we make in our business is always based on how we can maximise profit by reducing costs. That doesn't mean we run everything using free software or basic equipment, it means that every decision is based on the best return on our investment.

At times, your business will require significant investment for growth. The Experts is currently experiencing this. We've hired several new team members and incurred the associated costs. This is only possible because we've been frugal in the past, keeping costs to a minimum, building cash reserves, and knowing that there will be times in the future when we need to invest. That wouldn't be possible if we'd been unwise with the money we have.

It's easy to be tempted by a Mac Pro costing £15,000, when a Mac mini costing £3,000 will do the job. Or perhaps you're tempted to spend £3,000 a month on a cool studio space that looks good on social media, but you can do an equally good job for free from home.

Don't be tempted to spend money you don't need to spend. Think about it: in the two transactions above, I've shown that's £48,000 in one year you don't need to spend! That could be the deposit on the house you've always wanted.

You may be reading this and think I live like Scrooge, penny pinching and existing on bread and water. On the contrary, my family has a fantastic standard of living. We are debt free and have savings. When tax bills come, we have the cash to pay them. If ever there's an issue like the washing machine blowing up, we know we have the cash to fix it or buy a new one. We don't want for anything. Furthermore, if we see need elsewhere, then we are able to show generosity without having to worry about it.

All of this is possible because the businesses are run with maximum efficiency. They are run to ensure they have profits to support the families who depend on them.

The "real" definition of profit is the money that's left over when all the bills are paid. If you are self-employed, that's your take home pay. I've seen too many people blow thousands on unnecessary expenses for their business while their families are barely scraping by. That's insanity!

How much do you need to make?

The best piece of financial advice I was given about running a business was to start with how much money I needed for my family to live on and work backwards from that. A financial plan for your business based on your personal wealth focuses the mind.

Don't run a business hoping to make enough to survive, base your finances on a plan to thrive.

I suggest you sit down and do these sums. These are examples based on living in the UK. Depending on where you live, the numbers could be better or worse.

- First, write down how much you want to earn per year
- Next, you need to add 30% to that number to cover tax
- If you live in a country where medical cover isn't free, then add a percentage for that
- Let's do some simple maths. Let's imagine the first number is £50,000. Add the tax pot - that's £15,000. If you need to cover medical care, let's call that another £5,000. We now have a total of £70,000
- Your business therefore needs to generate at least £70,000 in PROFIT (not turnover) to cover your personal expenses
- At this point you can figure out how much the business needs to turn over. In the scenario above, if you assume you'll take four weeks of vacation, then you have 48 weeks to make at least £70,000. With rounding up, your business needs to turnover £6,000 per month, or £1,500 per week. If you charge £500 per day, then you need to work at least three days per week, every week, to generate that
- So far, we've not taken a single expense into account
- Let's assume that banking, accountants and general running costs like phones etc, are £10,000 per year. You need to generate an additional £700 per month to cover that

- You may decide you want a new Mac Pro, a few mics, a new interface and some plugins. That could be around £25,000. Now you need to make nearly £9,000 per month in order to continue taking home what you need

But what if all that new gear won't add any more income to the company? What if you could do the same work without it?

Remember what I said earlier. Many of our clients don't care how we get results or the gear we use to do the work. You may have a concern that you'll miss out on work if you don't have certain things in place: a studio to record drums, for example, or certain software tools. But if you will only use those things a couple of times each year, that makes them a costly expense. It would be better to hire a studio to record drums. You can hire the tools you need for rare jobs. That's how builders and other trades do it because it's smart. They only hire a tool when they need it, and in many cases, this is costed into the job.

Look around your business and make a mental note of all the equipment you have that isn't used 80-90% of the time. Some of that equipment could have cost thousands of pounds. You don't use it most of the time, but it represents a couple of months of your mortgage, or several weeks where you don't have to work. Wouldn't you like to have that kind of freedom?

You may not have the latest computer, the coolest car or an office in the best part of town, but your family will be taken care of and you won't need to worry about your personal finances. I can't underline how important all this stuff is. I've seen too many businesses go bust and far too many families face crippling debt because a business owner didn't do their sums.

How to cut costs

Here are 8 ways to build a successful business without wasting money.

1. Work from home or rent a space in a facility

Many people now work from home. Gone are the days of having a flash facility, because the numbers simply don't add up. It is true that impressions count, but make sure you are running the kind of audio business that needs an impressive facility. Many of us can work from home as, 99% of the time, our clients do not visit us. When I say "work from home" I know post mixers who are mixing top TV and films from a shed in their garden or from their basement. My physio works from a room in the basement of his house and the guy who got me my last mortgage from his dining room.

2. Rent equipment for projects

If you need something for just one project, rent it. A couple of days ago I was involved in a one-day film shoot. The gear we used was worth about £40,000. It included top cameras, prime lenses, lights and other equipment. The hire cost for the day was £550 and this cost was allocated to the job. When builders work on my house, they bring a lot of tools that they use every day, but if they need a digger or a specialist tool that costs thousands, they rent it and charge it to me. It's possible you might lose some work because you don't have a specific piece of gear, but don't lose profit by buying a piece that you can rent.

3. Borrow equipment for projects

Alternatively, if you have good friends in the same business, you may be able to borrow stuff for projects. When I lived in London, my long-time friend, James Ivey, and I lived a 10-minute drive from one another. We would often share gear and sometimes we would talk before we purchased things, to see what could work for both of us.

One small matter: make sure you insure anything you rent or borrow and treat it as if it were your own. If you get it back to the owner in the same condition as it arrived, you have more chance of being able to borrow it again.

4. Sell what you don't use

I'm amazed how much hardware and software I bought on whim that I used once then forgot about. If you are the same, put it on eBay or another selling site. Doing this, I managed to raise enough cash to buy something I really needed for another job.

5. If it's software then use a demo before you buy

When it comes to software, use a demo before you buy the product, and make sure you really need it. A lot of software companies offer time-limited or restricted demos of their software. This will usually give you enough opportunity to find out if you really need it, or to get the project finished.

6. Buy the right specification in the first place

One way to save money is to spend more in the first place. Buy computers for growth. In other words, don't just buy what you need now, buy what you'll need for the next phase of growth. Yes, it costs more now, but a lot less than buying, selling and buying again. It's the same for many other things like power tools or gym equipment. Cheap may seem a great way to save money, but it's not if you have to buy a better one later on.

7. Turn off equipment and lights

Depending on the gear you have and where you are in the world, air conditioning and heating costs can be huge. Save the planet and your pennies by turning off stuff when you are not using it.

8. Buy used gear

Like cars, buying equipment from new can often mean paying more than you have to. I often hear people cite the "I can write it off as a tax deduction" line. Well, that's a good theory, but it only works if you are making profit in the first place.

At the start of this chapter I mentioned that many people who now run businesses never intended to, becoming "accidental business owners". That may be the story so far, but if you've not paid attention to the money and the need for profit, perhaps this is a wakeup call. Pay attention to what you spend and the profit left. Otherwise, what began as a dream could end as a nightmare.

FINAL QUESTION

What could you stop spending money on today that wouldn't affect your business?

More Heat Than Light

QUICK TAKEAWAY
"More heat than light"
It's easy to think that busyness and activity are the
same as progress. They are not.
Make sure you work with the kind for people who make
the biggest impact, not the most noise.

"It is not enough to be busy; so are the ants.
The question is: What are we busy about?"
Henry David Thoreau

"Look busy the boss is coming!" is a popular joke that's
been doing the rounds for years. Someone once
developed a computer app that allowed you to hit a key
if the boss was approaching your workstation and it
displayed a complex spreadsheet on screen, to make it
look like you were working hard!

I'm sure you've also come across those people who
always seem to be incredibly "busy". Some have shared
images of their unread emails running into the thousands
on social media, like it's a badge of honour.

They are always telling everyone how busy they are
(normally with something "important"), but try and pin
them down and it's a different story.

Does he ever go to Tesco?

In the mid 80s, when I worked in music retail, I recall a conversation that took place between me, my boss and a mutual friend. Our mutual friend was in a rock band and was hoping to make it big as the next Foreigner or Toto.

The music store we worked in was very relaxed and often customers or friends (not mutually exclusive) would drop in for a cup of tea and a chat.

It was a warm Spring morning, the sun was out and Dave (name changed) came bounding into the shop. A vivacious and fun guy, life was rarely dull when he was around.

My boss, Nick, asked him what he'd been doing that day. I think the reply was something to do with him visiting a studio, having a meeting with a record company and other glamorous Rockstar type activities. We listened to his latest "shaggy dog" story and once he was bored, he said his goodbyes and left.

After he'd gone, Nick turned to me and asked,

"Do you think he ever goes to Tesco and buys a tin of beans?"

I laughed, knowing what he meant. Did he ever do anything mundane and normal like the rest of us mere mortals?

It's tempting to ham things up, to exaggerate, but in business what matters isn't the amount of activity you generate or how good your stories are - it's results that matter.

Wasting energy

I once had a weekly meeting with a client for a period, and each time I dreaded it.

It wasn't the client or the work that troubled me, it was one of the team members who would be on the call.

The problem was a simple one. Each call would move at a lightning pace and much of the conversation was taken up with this guy talking about his amazing ideas, his past successes, and how busy he was making things happen.

The problem was that each week, nothing really changed. If we suggested ideas, he had done them before, only better. If we tried to examine the success of current ideas, he quickly moved the discussion on. There seemed to be no way to uncover what was working and no evidence to support his claims of success.

This client was spending money with us to do marketing, so imagine when the company you've hired for marketing suggests that you stop spending the money...

...which is what I did.

I couldn't, in all good conscience, allow the spending to continue with little or no results.

A few months later I got a call from the CEO of the company to tell me that this member of his team was moving on. I wasn't surprised. Apparently, the situation had come to a head. We talked for some time about it and I said,

"I think the problem was there was more heat than light with him."

Heat isn't a bad thing if you want to warm up a room. But it's no use if you're trying to *light* a room.

"When an incandescent bulb is hooked up to a power supply, the electric current passes through a metal filament (usually tungsten), heating it until the filament is so hot that it glows. As the electrons move, they bump into the metal atoms of the filament. The energy of each collision vibrates the atoms and heats them up, eventually producing light. Only 10% of the energy used by an incandescent bulb is converted to light; the other 90% is lost as heat. The tray model represents the collisions between the electrons and the atoms of the filament... Since LEDs use electricity more efficiently than the other two types of bulb (they convert about 90% of it to light), they require much less energy to produce the same amount of light as incandescent or fluorescent bulbs."[21]

[21] The Pennsylvania State University

It's important to make sure that the energy expended running our business activities is used as efficiently as possible. The above light bulb example shows that you can get the same result by using 80% less energy. Heat is the by-product of an inefficient light bulb. With people, wasted energy manifests itself as busyness and noise, with little or no results.

First, let's consider why this happens, and secondly, how we can put in checks and balances to prevent it.

The right person

Many years ago, Willow Creek Community Church, a large church based in the USA, became known globally for pioneering "The Network Course".

The aim of the course was to help members of churches find their place of service within a community. The details of the course aren't important, but its central principle stuck with me:

'The right person in the right place for the right reason.'

This phrase is helpful because it sums up the three most important things to consider when selecting a person for a task:

- Competence
- Context
- Motivation

One of the first toys babies get is often a version of the wooden blocks and holes game. You know, each block is a certain shape, such as a square, a star, a circle, and the stand has corresponding holes they fit into. As an adult looking on, you watch as your child tries to put the star block into the circle hole or (like the old adage) a square peg in a round hole. Your instinct is to jump in and help, but you know it's not just about the solution, it's about problem solving, learning to explore and play.

In business, it's vital to find the right person to fit into a role, then empowering them to do it. I'm convinced it's essential, both for the wellbeing of the individual and the efficiency of a team, to have people who have the skills, the experience, and also the chemistry.

The kind of behaviour exhibited by the member of staff in my opening story could easily be attributed to nothing more than a big ego. Some people just like the sound of their own voice and want to be the centre of attention. But in many cases, all that noise is just an attempt to cover up their lack of ability. It's hard to admit we can't do something; that we've taken on a job we can't do well. The truth is, some people perform brilliantly in an interview, but are a terrible hire.

If you don't want more heat than light, it's crucial to get the right people in the right place for the right reason.

One of the most tempting things during the recruitment process is to think that just because someone has the right skills, they will be the perfect fit. However, they may have appropriate skills but lack experience of your industry. Or, they may have both the skills and experience, but the chemistry isn't right.

If we get this wrong, it can really upset the balance of an entire team. In some cases, the wrong hire can be worse than not hiring anyone. It can set teams and projects back weeks, months or even years.

Taking on the wrong work

You can also apply this principle to yourself if you are running a one-person business. There will invariably be times when you want to take on more work, and you are tempted to take on projects for which you lack either the skills, experience or chemistry.

You may have the right skills, but no experience of the sector. You may have both the skills and experience, but your gut tells you there's a disconnect between you and the client; it could be a difference in values or just that there's no personal chemistry.

It's hard to let go of what looks like the perfect job for you. In your heart you know you could probably do the job, but the fact is, someone else can do it better. They are a better fit.

Don't be the child trying to force the wrong piece into the wrong hole.

Specifications protect everyone

This mismatch can easily create friction, and that generates heat rather than light. Therefore, it's essential to nail down the specifications, values and expectations around any kind of contract, be it for a job or a project.

If you spend any time on social media groups or forums, you'll know there is a question that crops up time and again. It goes something like, "I've just finished the project and the client is asking for 'X', what should I do?"

If we get everything in writing before we start work, there is less chance of surprises cropping up for either party during the project. The same is true when working with other people, be they staff or contractors.

Get it in writing.

Data doesn't lie

I take far less of a day-to-day role in my company Production Expert these days. I'm certainly less active in the editorial aspect of the business. The role of a CEO is mostly leadership, helping to ensure the ship stays on course.

This means that much of my time is spent looking at either analytical or financial data. It's not what I'd *like* to do - I much prefer the creative aspect of the company - but it's the data that helps steer the ship.

Data doesn't lie.

Someone might tell me how much interest an article has received, then I look at the data and it tells me that's not true. Data tells me what platform readers are viewing the website on, and this helps determine if we should concentrate on the desktop or mobile development of the websites. Data tells me what *kind* of content people are reading, and this has informed decisions to kill certain aspects of our operation that were costly to maintain but didn't convert into readers. Data tells us what makes money and what doesn't.

It's never been easier to gather data about your business. Software is more powerful and cost effective than ever, and in some cases it's free.

If you spend money on things like Facebook advertising or Google Adwords, they will report on the results of each campaign, so you can see what ROI (return on investment) you are achieving. Free mailing systems like Mailchimp have powerful reports to show you who opened your emails, which emails people read, and what links in the email they clicked on. This makes it easier to target the right customers with the right information.

And, of course, most banks have apps that will show you what money is coming in and where you are spending it. There are also several powerful accounting packages, such as Freshbooks, Xero and Quickbooks, that can help you analyse your profit and loss.

In order to ensure you are creating more light than heat, you need data to inform those decisions. Without it you are sailing blind. Your decisions have no proof to back them up and before you know it your business is in a drift - or worse, dead in the water!

FINAL QUESTIONS

Are you generating heat or light?
How do you know what is happening?

Keep the Main Thing
the Main Thing

QUICK TAKEAWAY
"Keep the main thing the main thing"
It's tempting to think diversification will win you more business, but sometimes it will be a distraction and weaken your offering.

"Most people have no idea of the giant capacity we can immediately command when we focus all of our resources on mastering a single area of our lives."
Tony Robbins

I was out walking the dog when I got a call from a friend who had been offered an opportunity to join an accountancy firm as a partner. He wanted my advice on what I thought of the offer. Should he take it or pass?

He explained they were a successful accountancy practice who were considering moving into a new type of work. Within minutes, I must have put ten questions to him about what the company was proposing.

I asked him what size the market was, how many were already working in it. I asked about the average size of contract and how long each contract took from start to finish. I asked if they had a business plan for the idea.

I wonder what your questions would have been, knowing that was the company's plan? The most important question for me was a simple one: *why?*

Why would a successful accountancy firm want to move into a new area of work where they had no previous experience or track record? He surmised that it was because a lot of other companies in the sector were doing it. As I made clear in the chapter Seven Dogs Chasing the Same Cat, ubiquity isn't always a recipe for success.

Don't follow every trend

Whenever we see businesses in our space following a new trend, it's easy to think we are missing out. What if they know something we don't? What if this idea really takes off and our business is left behind?

These are reasonable questions to consider. It's right to keep an eye on trends, to see the direction of travel in a particular business sector.

When the Experts started over a decade ago, most of the alternative sources of information and news were print magazines. For publishers in this sector, magazines were their primary business and web was often an afterthought. This was understandable, as print was the established medium. Bloggers were considered fringe and certainly no threat to journalism. At best we were graffiti artists with punctuation. Now, most of those who were strong in magazines have either moved to the web or closed down.

However, it's also smart to keep *the main thing, the main thing*. There is great strength in focus. Focus is knowing what to say yes to and what to ignore.

Why focus matters

The first reason why focus matters is that it is a powerful selling point.

Consider this: you have a beautiful vintage Ferrari in your garage that needs some work done. Do you take it to any mechanic who works on all makes of car, or do you take it to the vintage Ferrari expert who has a reputation for being the best? My guess is you'll want the vintage Ferrari expert.

There's a reason for this. You know they earned their reputation by focusing on just *one thing*.

As time goes on, focus becomes the marketing equivalent of perpetual motion. They are the expert, so they get the work. In time, they may be the only one doing that type of work, then they can charge what they like.

There's an unlikely hit show on UK TV called *The Repair Shop*. It's a BBC production based on a simple premise. People bring in items that belonged to members of their family over generations, which are in dire need of repair. The items can range from the sign from a village hall, to a portrait of their mother, a bike, or a pinball machine. Most of the items are vintage and/or rare.

As each person arrives with their heirloom, they are introduced to the person best equipped to restore the item. There are no generalists, every single person has a skill that you wouldn't imagine is in need. How often does one need a book rebinding using the traditional method? Or how often does someone need an old glass barbershop sign restoring? Enough to keep these people in work! Furthermore, I imagine that because they are so specialised, there are only a handful of people in the country with those skills.

Hedging your bets

When I started Sociatech, it was important to quickly get some work. Like many with a new business, I took on all sorts of work just to get the bills paid. After all, only an idiot would turn down work.

The trouble with that approach was that a lack of focus and commitment to one speciality created two problems.

The first problem was that Sociatech wasn't really known for any kind of specialism. The portfolio of work lacked consistency. "I do a bit of this and a bit of that" is hardly a compelling sales proposition.

When potential clients asked me what I did, I would make a very generalised pitch. It was far less compelling than me saying we were specialists in one particular thing.

Secondly, like a self-fulfilling prophecy, because I wasn't concentrating on one thing, it meant I wasn't becoming good at one thing.

Nailing the company's colours to the mast and saying *this is the one thing we do* changed everything.

Now, we are a specialist marketing agency for the music and audio technology sector. You can count the people who have that as their job title in the world on the fingers of one hand. Better still, I'm pleased to call most of them my friends.

This means that our clients know what our focus is, and we know what we need to excel at.

If you want us to sell the new model BMW, we haven't got a clue. If you want us to come up with a product launch for a new lawn mower, we've got nothing.

What we *don't do* matters as much as what we do

However, if you want us to come up with a product launch for a new piece of music software, that's us. We know the product, the technology and the people who use it. We know the people who will endorse it and those who will write the reviews. This is because it's *all* we do.

It can be frightening to focus on just one thing, but the most compelling part of our pitch to potential new clients is telling them what we *don't* do.

I'll say, "We won't be selling a mixing desk today, a car the next day, and a sofa the next. All we do is music technology!"

This focus also means I know what to do to get better:
- Read books and websites about this subject
- Make contact with people in this sector
- Learn everything about the gear in this sector

I don't read gardening books or browse furniture production websites. That's not my focus. I immerse myself in the industry I work in, because that's how I stay sharp.

10,000 hours

At this point I could start citing the 10,000-hour theory, made popular by author Malcolm Gladwell. But those who conducted the research that Gladwell based his theory on suggest his analysis is flawed. His theory was based on a 1993 paper written by Anders Ericsson, a Professor at the University of Colorado.

Ericsson felt that Gladwell misinterpreted the research and didn't take into account that the 10,000 hours number was an average, and that some in the study had spent significantly fewer hours perfecting their skill.

Whatever the number, it is clear that whether it's the amount of hours or the quality of the practice, to become a master of something takes focus and effort.

Maintaining focus in the modern world is tough. In his book, *Here Comes Everybody*, Clay Shirky says the problem is not so much the amount of information rushing towards us, but our ability to filter it.

We need to make smart choices about where we place our focus and, in many cases, focus is found by cutting things out. I stopped reading the news for a significant length of time, because when I analysed my day, I could spend over an hour consuming it. Much of it, I couldn't do anything about and didn't need to know. Yet, it took up my time, my mental energy, and often took away my peace of mind.

Good ideas are equally tempting. I have moments when I'd like to learn how to code, for instance. But to get to any level of competence would take a great deal of time - time I could spend being better at what I already know. I can't be top of my game if I allow other things to steal my time and my focus. Keeping the main thing, the main thing, is about making choices. Choices about what we are going to excel at and how we intend to make sure we maintain that.

FINAL QUESTIONS
How focused is your business?
Are you being tempted to hedge your bets?

Pay the Good Ones Fast

QUICK TAKEAWAY
"Pay the Good Ones Fast"
Look after those who look after you.
There are times when they need to make a choice;
make sure the choice is you.

"You're lovin' gives me a thrill
But you're lovin' don't pay my bills
Now give me money
That's what I want."
The Supremes

You should always steer clear of any takeaway food outlet that answers the phone with the line, "The driver's just left..."

I had to stop using our local taxi firm because each time I called to chase a late booking, the person on the phone would tell me they were just leaving.

Lateness makes my blood boil. It takes all my effort not to start berating a cab driver when they arrive late. Part of me wants to ask if their time is more valuable than mine. However, it usually happens when my wife and I are going out to dinner and her death stare is enough to shut me up.

It's said that the most common lie in business is "the cheque's in the post". This is much harder to pull off these days with digital payment systems, but it seems that some people will find any excuse not to pay.

In my earlier years, it wasn't always easy to impress Dad. Whether it was a car I'd bought, a house, or a job, Dad would usually find something that I could have done better.

As I got older, and even more so once Dad had retired, it seemed my business ventures were something Dad was proud of. Even though Dad had retired from work, he would still take a keen interest. He would ask how it was going and as I told him he would comment on how pleased he was with the success.

My accountant of many years was introduced to me by my Dad. He had looked after Dad's business and personal tax for years. Dad didn't stand for any messing around, so there was no higher recommendation.

As tax season came around, Dad would ask if Graham, the accountant, had looked after me. He always did, making sure no more tax was paid than was legally necessary.

When I told him it was all good, Dad would ask if I had paid him. The answer was always the same, "Yes, Dad." To which Dad would reply, "Good, always pay those who look after you fast."

The reason Dad said this was two-fold.

First, if someone had looked after you by doing good work, making them wait for their money was an insult. As far as Dad was concerned, the best way to thank them was to pay them fast. It's just the right thing to do.

The second reason was that it engendered goodwill and loyalty. There was a greater chance they'd be motivated to look after the person who looks after them.

Million-dollar baby

One of Sociatech's clients was introduced to us about two years ago. When they came to us, they were turning over about $300,000 a year.

One of the things that gets me out of bed in the morning is seeing potential, then helping someone to realise it - especially someone who you can see deserves success.

A few months after taking the client on we had the chance to meet up in London for an event. Afterwards, we joined a group of colleagues for dinner. As we were walking back from the restaurant, I was talking with the client and he asked me what potential I believed his business had.

I didn't need long to answer the question because I had already considered it beforehand.

"I think we should pass one million dollars turnover per annum in the next two years," I told him.

My client said nothing. That meant one of two things: he was either shocked and excited or thought I was full of crap.

At the end of 2020 we passed the one million dollar annual turnover mark as promised. It was an exciting moment to achieve such a landmark for a small, growing business.

That client pays his invoices every month in minutes after I send them. He is such a fast payer I joke with him about how slow he is to pay. Once, an invoice got lost in the system and he was so angry and disappointed. He told me he felt he had broken his unblemished track record.

What's most important though is this: the client could express all the thanks in the world about our service and performance, but if he didn't pay his bills they would be hollow words.

The greatest way to thank people who do good work for you is to pay them and pay them fast. The good news is that Sociatech and the Experts are both fortunate enough to have clients who are fast payers. Our bad debt is almost non-existent. I never take this for granted, as I know other companies struggle to get paid in a reasonable time.

You may be wondering if I asked this client what he was thinking the day I said we could get to a million dollars in two years.

"Did you think I was full of crap?'" I asked him on a call one day. He took too long to answer, so I laughed, knowing the truth.

The quickest payment in the history of the world

In the midst of the Covid19 pandemic, just before Christmas 2020, I was asked by a client to arrange a film shoot in London for a new product promo video we were working on. I'm based in Ireland and at the time, lockdown rules prevented me from being on the shoot.

I knew that wasn't a problem as I could call a trusted guy, Brian, to handle the directing and manage the shoot for me. Brian could be me if I wasn't there, all it would need from me was a couple of meetings with him and a clear shooting script. Armed with those things, I knew he would deliver.

I needed actors for the shoot too, so I asked trusted people who they recommended. Within a couple of days, I had names, had contacted them, and they were in.

The restrictions of lockdown meant we needed to shoot on a Saturday and, as it was so late in the year, we would be shooting a couple of weeks before Christmas. Who wants to work on a Saturday so close to Christmas? To my delight, all of the team said yes.

Brian was available and agreed to handle the shoot. He suggested an assistant to help him on the day. This was a sensible idea, so I agreed that addition, even though it wasn't in the original shoot budget.

The film shoot went ahead without a hitch. The day it happened I was at home in Ireland, hanging Christmas lights on the outside of my house. This was interspersed with two or three calls with Brian, who was sending over footage examples for me to approve. The actors did exactly what we hoped for, as did Brian and his assistant. It couldn't have gone better. I knew that within a couple of days, a portable hard drive would arrive with all the rushes from the shoot so I could edit them. My trust in all involved had been rewarded and I had peace of mind.

As soon as the invoices arrived, I paid them. One of the invoices arrived while I was out walking my dog. Thanks to my bank having a cool iPhone app, I was able to pay it whilst stood on a beach looking out across Belfast Lough. Within seconds of paying it, I got a text from the actor. It read, "Quickest payment in history of world! Hopefully meet you in REAL LIFE one day."

I'm not sure if it was the quickest payment in the history of the world, but the text spoke for itself. By paying as soon as I could, I created goodwill between me and someone who, days earlier, had gotten me out of a hole.

We should pay people promptly because it's the right thing to do, but the pay-off is the creation of goodwill between you and someone you may need help from again.

None of us know the circumstances of the people we hire to do work for us. They may be struggling to make ends meet. If it's a start-up business, it's highly likely that things are tough at the start. They may be facing all sorts of financial challenges.

Looking down the barrel of a gun

I remember exactly where I was when I called my wife, Anna, to tell her about my debt crisis. It was the Autumn of 2007. It was a dark, wet, Saturday evening and I was stood in the front room of a house rental we had recently moved into in South East London. Anna wasn't home, so we spoke on her mobile.

I had just added up all my debts, acquired for various reasons. Some were the impact of a divorce and some arose through thoughtless spending. I was in a mess.

The number was big. At that time, it far exceeded my annual income. It was an accumulation of credit cards, finance agreements and bank loans. I felt like I was staring down the barrel of a loaded gun, with no way out of the mess.

Over the years, Mum and Dad had been enormously generous to me, but this was a problem of my own making and one I needed to sort out myself.

"Anna," I said, choked with fear and shame and wondering how I'd get out of this mess. "I owe a lot of money and I don't know what I'm going to do."

She could hear the emotion in my voice and, without missing a beat, she calmly and lovingly said, "Don't worry, honey, we will sit down when I get home and work out how to fix this."

When Anna got home, we sat down and worked out a plan to clear the debt. The following Monday morning I started calling credit card companies and the other companies to explain my situation. I entered into arrangements to pay. This is where the interest on the debt is frozen and you make a regular monthly payment to clear the remaining balance. By the end of that day, everyone had been contacted and there was a plan to clear the debt.

It wasn't fast or easy. For several years we lived having just £30 of spare cash per week to buy food and other household essentials. All non-essential spending stopped. Any spare cash was used to settle the debts.

Just as I recall the day when I faced the enormity of my own personal debt, I also recall the day when I was debt free. On April 11, 2013, I posted on Facebook:

"It took me 5 years of hard work, but as of today I am completely debt free! Let's have a drink!"

It was a long journey and a huge life lesson - one that has stayed with me ever since. To this day, other than the mortgage on our house, we don't take on any kind of debt, credit cards or otherwise. We also have savings for when we need to make large purchases or the unexpected happens, like the washing machine blows up.

Dad once said to me, "Never lend people to people who are in debt." Instead he told me to give them the money they needed as a gift. They couldn't afford to pay the money back in any case, and a loan would be just another burden to them. Having been there and faced the huge burden of debt, I know Dad was right.

I know what debt feels like. It's frightening. It fills you with shame and makes you feel trapped.

The cost of late payments

The Federation of Small Businesses (FSB) estimate that around 50,000 businesses close every year due to late payments. According to the US website Business Insider, 82% of small businesses experience cash flow problems and 29% run out of cash altogether. One study by the US Bank claims a staggering 82% of business fail due to cashflow mismanagement.

It's easy to think of a business as a faceless entity, but for every small business owner a late payment is the inability to pay rent or the mortgage. It can be as real as not being able to buy food and clothes for their family, or worse critical medication.

It is therefore essential to make sure we pay as fast as we can. Sometimes you may be waiting for payment yourself. If that is the case, then I recommend two things. Make sure you tell those involved in the project this will be the case before they take on the work. Secondly, as soon as you get paid, pay them first. Simon Sinek sums it up perfectly with the title of his book, *Leaders Eat Last*.

Rubbing salt in the wounds

A few years ago, I found one of my businesses with the worst kind of bad debt. The company who owed us money had gone bust. Unless you are really lucky, then the chance of ever seeing the money again is somewhere between zero and never.

Businesses fail for all sorts of reasons and this one found themselves in a perfect storm of events that forced them to shut their doors. I spoke with my contact there who explained the situation. He was deeply apologetic and hoped someday to be able to put the matter right.

Within weeks of this event, pictures began appearing on social media of the managing director of the failed company on an amazing foreign holiday, and then enjoying a lavish birthday party. I know how companies work. As the director of a limited company, the debt wasn't his; it wasn't him personally who owed me the money, but the company. However, as you can imagine, it left a nasty taste in my mouth and a lasting impression. The bad debt meant I couldn't take a vacation or have a party. He hadn't done anything wrong legally, but I felt he'd rubbed salt in the wounds.

I still see this person. I hold no lasting ill-will towards him or his business enterprises, but as leaders we need to take care. We can't, on the one hand, withhold payments or worse not pay at all, creating hardship, and on the other hand live a publicly lavish lifestyle. It's simply not a good look and will earn you a reputation that might harm you chances of hiring talented people in future.

Get paid fast

I was wondering how best to end this chapter. It's aimed at those who need to pay bills, but often we don't because we are waiting to be paid. Some of you will be reading this chapter and be dealing with the hardship of invoices that remain unpaid.

With those people in mind, I thought I would offer some practical steps to getting paid fast.

- Make invoicing a priority. Do it as soon as a job is done, don't wait until the end of the month
- If you can get a deposit up front, then do it. If nothing else, this will help pay for the cost of the work

- Don't offer payment terms, only discuss them when asked. Unless otherwise agreed, it's payment on completion of the work
- If possible, don't release the final work until the payment has been made, but make sure this condition is in your terms before you start the job. In some cases, the final work is the only guarantee of you getting paid
- Make it easy for your clients to pay you using systems like Paypal, Stripe and Wise
- Invest in an accounting application such as Freshbooks, Xero or Quickbooks. These make invoicing and getting paid super easy
- Chase any late payments with gentle reminders by email. If that doesn't work, then call the client and ask if there is a reason for the delay

It's important to keep the cash coming in. The statistics for small businesses are stark. It might be the difference between success and failure, so don't let it get out of hand.

If you sit on money you owe for work done, then pay as soon as you have it. This is the best way of saying thank you and it engenders loyalty.

FINAL QUESTIONS

Is there someone you need to pay now?
Is it time to get your invoicing into
shape so you can get paid fast?

Measles or Mumps?

QUICK TAKEAWAY
"Measles or Mumps?"
People don't catch what you say, they catch who you are, so be sure to set a good example as a leader.

"A good example is the best sermon."
Benjamin Franklin

It was the early 2000s and a company I was running at the time was moving into a new office. It was a hectic morning as desks were moved in and computers set up. Several of the team were in the office and something was going wrong.

My assistant at the time was setting up the computers. It involved Windows computers, servers and networks, but he was an incredibly capable guy; we were in safe hands.

It was an events company and the move was happening in the midst of a busy bookings period. The longer the computer systems were down, the greater the chance of us losing business.

I can't recall exactly what was happening, but I was getting stressed about the lack of progress. At some point I asked why things were being done a certain way. My assistant told me what the issue was and why he advised we do it that way.

The discussion continued and my stress levels continued to rise. At some point I snapped. In front of several staff I said to him, "It's my business and I want it done my way!"

My business partner was also in the room and he asked me to step outside with him. When we were out of earshot he said to me, "Russ, what you said in there... it's technically true, but you *never* say it."

He was right. I'd been arrogant and in a moment of frustration I'd let myself down in front of my entire team. I'd committed the cardinal sin of management and leadership: never rebuke someone in front of others. My partner could have done the same to me, but he took the right path.

I apologised to my assistant and to all those in the room. My outburst was uncalled for and not a good way to motivate the team. It certainly meant I'd lost some ground in terms of respect, and I would need to work hard to get it back.

What will they catch?

Here's a question: if your kid tells you they have measles, but they actually have mumps, what do you catch?

The answer is mumps, of course, because you don't catch what they say they have, you catch what's inside of them.

People catch who we are, not what we say.

Peter Economy writing for Inc. says,

"If you're a leader, your employees are watching every move you make. It's not because they don't trust you, and it's not because they want to keep track of your every move. The reason your people watch you closely is that they want to know if what you say and what you do are the same - that is, that you walk the talk."[22]

Leading by example is powerful. It's not just important when you are dealing with internal team issues, but also when you need to take your business in a new direction.

A few years ago, the Experts team had flown to my home in Northern Ireland for a few days of appraisal, brainstorming and planning. We sat together looking through the data on visitors to the site, and it did not make good reading. Visitors were dropping at about 10% per month. Given this trajectory, if something didn't happen fast, we were facing an existential crisis.

We talked about why we thought the visits were dropping and discussed the internal and external factors we believed were contributing to the woeful numbers.

---

[22] Peter Economy, Inc.

Once the meeting was over, I spoke with Mike Thornton, my friend and fellow owner of the Experts company. I've worked with Mike for around 8 years, and I can't think of anyone I'd rather share the journey with. While we have very different styles of leadership, we always agree on vision; we just sometimes have different ways of getting there.

We'd looked through the data and now it was time to act. As we talked, we came up with a plan to turn things around. It was an ambitious plan that would mean some significant changes for the whole team.

The next time we sat down with the team we had a plan to share. If this plan was going to work, Mike and I had to believe in it, we couldn't fake it. We did believe in the plan and during that meeting we cast the vision for the team, who all got behind it with enthusiasm.

The good news is, the plan worked. Within months, we had not only stopped the slide but added significant growth. It took effort on the part of the whole team, who worked their socks off to make it happen, but they needed a plan to believe in - one they could throw themselves into.

Every business has challenges; times when it looks like everything is falling apart and that things may not work out. At these moments, leadership is essential. We have to come up with a vision and either lead it ourselves or guide an entire organisation to success.

Come on, you can do it!

You may recall the scenes in the movie *Rocky*, where his coach Mickey is pushing him hard, willing him on to win. Leadership is all about that. It's about instilling belief in those who may not believe in themselves, picking them up when they fall down and showing them the way when they lose it.

Peter Drucker put it this way:

'Leadership is not magnetic personality, that can just as well be a glib tongue. It is not 'making friends and influencing people', that is flattery. Leadership is lifting a person's vision to higher sights, the raising of a person's performance to a higher standard, the building of a personality beyond its normal limitations.'[23]

I find myself doing this often with our team or clients.

It's an essential part of business, because sometimes the only one who has faith in it working is you. Believe it or not, sometimes you need to speak to *yourself* and give yourself a good talking to. Leadership starts with us.

In the words of Eleanor Roosevelt. "One's philosophy is not best expressed in words; it is expressed in the choices one makes... and the choices we make are ultimately our responsibility."

---

[23] Peter F. Drucker, Management: Tasks, Responsibilities, Practices

As one wise person said, "You can't lead anything else if you can't lead your own life."

Don't expect someone who can't manage their personal finances to be able to take care of the finances of a business. Don't expect someone who can't hold down relationships in their personal life to act differently in a corporate environment. There's not a work version of you and a home version, one is just an extension of the other.

Attending to oneself is the first step in effective leadership.

Why all this talk about leadership?

So, why all this talk about leadership in a business book? Isn't this only important if you're running a big corporation?

Not at all.

The very fact you've started a business is an act of leadership. You came up with an idea then acted on it.

Leadership is seeing something that doesn't yet exist and believing it will come to pass.

Even if your business is just you, leadership is essential because every day you need to lead your business. No one else is going to do it.

If you handle projects like a video shoot or an album recording or a house build... these things require leadership as well as management. It requires belief and conviction in what the final outcome will be; that things are going to work. You have to be able to convey that to everyone else involved in making it happen.

Seeing things not yet in existence

In 1998, I joined with my then business partner to put on a large conference event in Kent. The plan was to hold it in the year 2000. It required building an entire conference infrastructure large enough for several thousand people to attend over several days. There was no suitable venue to make that happen in the area.

When we began, we had nothing. We eventually found a venue normally used as an agricultural showground, but we needed a place for seminars with keynote speakers. We needed accommodation, food venues and toilets. We needed money!

The moment I stepped onto that field, I could see the entire thing, as if I was watching the whole conference in virtual reality. At this point we were two years away and far from making it real.

The next two years were tough, putting the whole thing together. We had to source contractors, finance and specialists who could help us put the whole thing on.

One of the hardest things was trying to explain to other people what we were doing. Some would listen with genuine interest and *want* to get it, but they didn't.

Eventually, we got it over the finish line and the event went live in 2000 with several thousand attendees over a week. My lasting memory of that first year was walking around the event, speaking with people who had shared the journey with us in the preceding two years. Time and again they would say to me, "*This* is what you meant!" They had finally realised what the vision was and what we had been working towards all along.

Starting a business or even a new project requires seeing things that don't yet exist. That's why they call it *vision*. It might be a movie you are working on, a film score, a building, or a new piece of software. Whatever it is, the first step is imagining what does not yet exist then making it happen.

The ultimate act of creativity

I can't think of any more creative process on the planet than leadership - the art of taking nothing and making it something. Can you imagine anything more exiting and exhilarating?

A word of warning

But there's a negative side to the power of leadership, as outlined in the opening words of this chapter. Leaders not only have the power to create but also destroy.

As the leader of your business, you create the culture, you set the tone and the temperature. That can be good or bad. As we've been exploring in this chapter, our actions speak louder than our words.

Have you ever noticed with some people that you can't hear what they are saying because *who they are* speaks so loudly? Their toxic personality cancels out anything good they say. It seems hollow at best and fake at worst.

As business leaders we need to pay careful attention to this truth and cultivate lives of integrity, where our actions match our words. Our team is watching, so are our customers, and the more influential you become the more they pay attention. It's sobering to consider.

That's why I'm cautious about those who want to run a personality-driven business. Taking that approach can be a liability as much as an asset.

If you use your personality to define your business' public persona, you need to take careful steps with everything you say and do. A misstep can undo months if not years of brand equity.

When I started the blog in 2008, I became aware that as it grew, I was seen as the face of the blog. In the early years, when it was just me, this was an inevitable fact, but as soon as the team grew, I worked hard to dispel that image.

It's not that I'm a bad person, but like everyone else, I'm a flawed human being and I make mistakes. I felt it unwise to have me as the face of the blog. Furthermore, the success was not just down to me, others deserved credit.

Some of my clients also take this approach, preferring to let their brand speak for itself and keeping their personality out of the picture. It's a wise approach and one I would recommend to anyone for the reasons outlined above.

You can't fake it

Business is about leadership, irrespective of the size of your company. It's about coming up with the idea, setting the direction and getting there.

I happen to think that running your own business is one of the hardest things to do. It means sleepless nights, worry about money, stress about deadlines, and hundreds of other challenges that come our way. Running a business is not for the faint hearted.

Leadership is an equally scary and, at times, incredibly lonely journey to walk.

One thing is certain, you can't fake leadership. It takes more than words. People are looking to you to show them the right way to go. It might be staff needing hope when the sales have dried up, or a client needing assurance that their project is in safe hands.

Measles or mumps? Whichever it is, people catch who you are and what you do - not what you say!

FINAL QUESTIONS

What do you find hardest about leadership?
What do you need to do to develop that part of you?

The Best is Yet to Come...

This book wasn't something I planned to write. As the title makes clear, when alive, Dad actively encouraged me not to bother writing a book. He saw it as a waste of time. Perhaps he'll be right?

I certainly didn't have "write a book" on my to-do list any time soon. What with running two businesses and home-schooling my daughter during lockdown, it wasn't as if I needed to fill my days with additional work.

Then, within days of getting sick, Dad died. He was normally bulletproof. In the past, even after several serious medical emergencies, days later Dad would walk out of hospital with a dismissive, "Don't worry about me."

On one such occasion I called my sister and said I was having a t-shirt made for him saying, "Officially Bulletproof" and we laughed. When I told people Dad was sick and it wasn't looking good, I expected to make an embarrassed retraction within the week. But it was not to be. Given Dad's track record, his death took our family by complete surprise.

Dad was gone.

Soon after, I started getting messages from people telling me how much they had recognised Dad's influence in my business life. Complete strangers who had never met Dad were quoting his one-liners back to me. It was then that I thought the best way to honour his legacy was in print.

This book hasn't been written with any wild notion of appearing in the New York Times bestseller list. I'm not expecting an invitation to present a TED Talk. I'm certainly not expecting to get rich from writing this book.

Here is my greatest hope...

You may have never known Dad, but even so, like many of those who contacted me after his death, you've been able to benefit from a little bit of Dad's wisdom in your life too.

It is my sincere hope that this book inspires you to become more than you ever expected to be.

That's how I feel about my life. I'm more than I expected to be. Despite the different things life has thrown at me, I'm incredibly lucky/blessed (whatever suits your world view) to be doing what I do... AND GETTING PAID TO DO IT!

How many people can say that?

I hope you are one of them. Or, if you're not one yet, that this book helps you to become so.

Dad was a huge Frank Sinatra fan. He even looked like him when he was younger.

Let's leave the final word to Frank... the best is yet to come!

Quick Additional Business Tips

Business Morning Health Check

Here's the morning health check I do each day on my business. It takes no more than 30 minutes, but I find it's essential to keep me on top of all those things that can get out of hand if left to mount up.

- Grab breakfast - I'm useless without fuel
- Check email. Sort them according to the Inbox Zero principle: *Do, Delegate, Defer, Delete.*

You can read more about this in "5 Business Tools That Help Me Manage My Business" at the end of this book.

- Check social media business accounts for activity that might need my attention. There won't be any messages because I use the message autoresponder tools they supply. This means anyone who tries to message my businesses over social media is directed to the contact forms on my website

- Check news and social media for stories that might impact my business. Sometimes it's information, other times inspiration. It can sometimes inform the work on the blog

- Check my business calendar to see what meetings I have AND more importantly what space I have to complete tasks.

- Check my personal calendar to make sure I don't miss any important family events such as child-care, school events or other things that could clash with my day

- Check the bank to see what payments have come in from clients. If any are late, I send a statement to the client as a gentle reminder. If they have paid, I thank them

- Check to see if there are any people who need paying and make sure I pay them

- Check the billing software to see what turnover has happened this month. I like to try and hit my income target by the 10th day of each month. This way I know whether I need to find more work or I can relax

- Check in on my businesses to see if there are things that I need to highlight with my team to fix. In retail they call this "walking the floor".

- Check in with team members to discuss any needs for the day. Let them know if I'm going to be unavailable due to meetings or work that needs my attention

- Attend to any regular tasks such as sending out newsletters or other business-generating activities

Take Care of the Money

Two events took place recently that give me the sense that far too many creatives still forget what makes them a professional.

The first was a link to story that appeared on my Facebook timeline entitled, "5 Things All Audio Professionals Should Know". It was a good list, but seemed to have one huge omission: there was no mention of money.

The second was that my wife booked a professional consultant to visit our house. On arrival I asked how much we were paying her for her service.

The consultant went coy and said, "I hate talking about money." So, as kindly as possible, I did a little consultation of my own. I explained how she needed to have that discussion before she left her office to visit us.

What if I had not accepted her rate for the job? What if I couldn't afford to pay it?

Having the discussion at that point was not appropriate. No one likes talking about money, but we have to get used to it.

The difference between professional and amateur

What makes you a professional? You get paid for doing what you do. That's the distinction between an amateur and a professional.

Too often the word "professional" is used unhelpfully as a status symbol; a badge designating expertise or experience. This has blurred its meaning.

Let's be clear, you might be the most knowledgeable and experienced person in your field of expertise, but if you don't get paid for what you do, then you're not a professional.

Show me the money

As a professional, you should never forget that you are getting paid for offering the service of your skills and expertise. With that in mind, there are a few things you should take note of:

- Make sure people know how much your services cost and when you need paying. Be clear about money before you even start the job
- Never apologise when asking for money. Being a professional means getting paid for the service you offer
- Make sure you stay on top of billing. No one will ask you for the invoice

- Make sure you chase the money you are owed. Few clients pay on time
- Remember to thank your clients when they pay you. They may be struggling for money themselves and a little gratitude goes a long way

Love is the reason, money is the way

You are quite likely doing the work you do because you love doing it. At least, I hope that's the case.

There are plenty of projects I've worked on over the years that I've been so honoured to be part of, I would have done the work for free. Some days I smile and think, "I'm getting paid for sitting here all day doing something I love."

That's fantastic. Not everyone can say the same thing. Many people work jobs they hate just to pay the bills, so to do something you love and get paid for it is a fantastic situation to find yourself in.

What makes you a professional is that you get paid for the service you offer. Don't confuse your motivation for *starting* your business with the reason you *run* your business. Love what you do, but if you're a professional then make sure you get paid for it.

5 Business Tools That Help Me Manage My Business

I'm a creative by nature, which means organisation and order doesn't come naturally to me. I'd do anything to avoid taking care of my accounts and completing my tax returns. However, as a small business owner, there are certain tasks I have to stay on top of if I don't want the business to go out of control.

Here are five software tools I use that I've found indispensable over the years. They are so easy and intuitive that even the most chaotic person can use them!

Freshbooks

Money is the lifeblood of any small business and bad cashflow can kill a business dead in its tracks. For several years now I've been using Freshbooks for staying on top of accounts. It enables you to bill and collect money with the minimum of fuss, and gives you access to several different payment gateways to make paying you easy for your clients (such as Paypal and Stripe).

One of the best features is time tracking, so you can make sure you bill your clients for all the work done on a project, down to the last minute. You can try it free for 30 days and professional plans start at about $15 per month. I love it!

https://www.freshbooks.com

Wise (Formerly TransferWise)

If you do business across countries and currencies, then you are often at the mercy of banks and their charging fees. Paypal can prove costly too. One of my suppliers recommended TransferWise to me, which aims to lower charges and use fair currency exchange rates. They use what they describe as "mid-band" exchange rates and charge around 0.5% or £2.00 under £400 as the transaction fee, which is amazing, especially when you compare it to our bank's fee of £10 to £22 per transaction.

You can have a personal or a business account with them and it works because you pay into a TransferWise account in your country, then pay your supplier from a TransferWise account in their country, bypassing the banks' transfer fees and charges.

https://wise.com

Polymail for Mac, Windows, iOS

Many small business owners are not good at time management and one place where this often shows is their email, evidenced by a huge unread message count and folders of unanswered emails.

I've tried time management applications and they don't help. In fact, they often make matters worse and pile on the guilt. I must have spent hundreds of pounds on them.

A few years ago, I was introduced to the concept of Inbox Zero, which uses mail to manage your time. It works by treating mail in the following way: every email is assigned one of the following actions:

- **Do.** Act upon it now. It's important and urgent, or so easy it can be acted upon quickly
- **Defer.** Set it aside for a later date. It needs acting upon, but not now
- **Delegate**. Forward it to a person who is better placed to deal with it
- **Delete**. It has no purpose and needs trashing

At the end of this process, the only things sitting in your Inbox are the things you need to complete today. The aim is to end up with nothing in your Inbox at the end of each day. Hence the term "Inbox Zero". The system is simple and liberating.

This is made easy using Polymail, a fantastic mail app that allows you to defer mail until a later date of your choosing. I don't use folders or rules - either there's stuff in my Inbox or it's deferred or archived. If I need to find an email, the powerful search facility means I have no need for endless folders to lose stuff in. It's changed my life. You don't need Polymail to use the Inbox Zero method, but I can't imagine doing it without.

Polymail has both free and paid options.

www.polymail.io

Calendly

If you are tired of the back and forth of arranging meetings then Calendly is a simple but useful tool that enables your clients to choose a time to meet, or even schedule a session with you. They don't need access to your calendar and don't see anything you want to keep private.

You can use either a freeform option, where they can book as much time as they like, or presets defined by you. I've opted for 15-, 25- and 50-minute slots. The latter gives me time to decompress after each meeting.

Calendly is a paid-for service if you want some key features, but they offer a free version too if you want to try it out.

https://calendly.com

Reclaim

If you have several Google accounts, for example a personal one and a business one, it can get complicated trying to arrange meetings for your business that don't conflict with your personal life.

Reclaim is genius. You connect it to your Google accounts, then it syncs your personal and business calendars. Even better, any personal events in your calendar just appear as "busy" to your clients. They don't see if you are going to the dentist or taking the kids to soccer.

But Reclaim doesn't stop there. It can manage your life by including things like lunch, decompression and downtime into your diary, but built around the events that are booked. In essence, it is like having your own personal assistant protecting you, but without the cost! At the time of writing Reclaim is free.

https://reclaim.ai

Dad's Story

Gordon William Hughes was born in Aston, Birmingham in 1932, just before the Second World War, to Fredrick and Lillian.

Dad didn't get the best start in life. His father died an alcoholic when Dad was in his teens and his mother was out working all day.

His formative years were a recipe for delinquency and failure, but Dad decided that his past was not going to determine his future.

An early indication of his attitude to discipline and hard work was a stint in the military doing National Service.

When entering the world of work, he was always open to trying out an idea to see if he could make it a success. He always worked for himself, choosing to try and make his own success.

During the early years of marriage, Dad had a café, then a window cleaning business. He had a stint at running a garden centre. This was years before garden centres were a thing!

Then, in the early 1980s, Dad decided to try selling insurance for a company called Abbey Life. He was now in his forties and something clicked. He was something of a rough diamond, compared to others in the company, but he soon forged ahead, selling millions of pounds worth of insurance. He became a member of the coveted Chairman's Club.

He expanded his work into commercial pensions and insurance, and set up an office with a team of staff.

We used to joke that Dad would be carried out of his office "in a coffin" because he loved his work. He continued running his successful insurance company until he sold the business and retired in his early seventies.

What was clear was that Dad's motivation for success was to build a safe and stable home for his family. During the early years of Dad's endeavours money was tight. Even though Mum and Dad told us it was a struggle, I don't think we were ever aware of that being the case.

However, once Dad found the thing he could flourish at, he made sure the family benefited. I recall us being the first family amongst all our friends to own a video recorder.

That said, because our parents had known what it was to live without, they were never ostentatious. If you met Dad in the street, you would never have known the wealth he had, and he certainly didn't see it as a reason to look down on others. He had little time for posers and treated those from the most humble backgrounds with as much respect as the wealthy people he mixed with in his working life.

Over the years, as we grew up, Dad continued to make sure we all benefitted from his success. He never spoilt us, but if we were ever in need, he would try to help.

For Dad, success wasn't the goal, it was the kind and generous acts he could do with that success. Now that's a lesson worth aspiring to!

Acknowledgments

I don't like the term "self-made man". I'm the result of so many interactions in my life, be they with people, poems, books, magazine articles, songs, TV shows or movies. Every one of those touch points is owed my gratitude.

Additionally, I am grateful to so many people who have inspired and enriched my life. I know I will miss many by trying to compile a list, so I ask for forgiveness from any I leave out.

To Seth Godin and James Clear, who have inspired and informed so much of what I do.

To my Experts business partner, Mike Thornton, for your wisdom and friendship and for being nothing like me.

To the many Experts who have contributed to the success of the blog - they run into the hundreds, but a special mention goes to Julian, James, Dan and Eric, who have shared a significant chunk of the journey.

To Jed, PJ and Tony for your friendship, support, wisdom and outstanding work with Sociatech.

To Tim Pettingale for being a great book editor and an even better friend.

To so many treasured friends, too numerous to mention.

To Jack, Daisy, Poppy, Lily and Aoife, the stars that light up my night sky. To my sisters Lesley, Claire and Paula.

And, of course, the two women in my life: Anna and Mum!

This is for all of you, but most of all for Dad. RIP.

About the Author

Russ Hughes is the Founder of Production Expert, a group of blogs for music and post-production professionals. Over the last decade it has become one of the leading industry websites with over 7 million visitors annually.

He is also the CEO of Sociatech, a global marketing agency for the music technology sector, working with some of the biggest brands in the industry. He has advised brands, both large and small, including Amazon, on effective blogging strategies to help create passionate brand advocates.

In his spare time, he likes to spend time with his family, walk his dog Buddy, and run.

https://www.russ-hughes.com

Made in the USA
Las Vegas, NV
25 April 2021